Three Ring Circus

Life as a Missionary Kid in a Family of 11

Luke Gray

WestBow Press books may be ordered through booksellers or by contacting:

WestBow Press
A Division of Thomas Nelson & Zondervan
1663 Liberty Drive
Bloomington, IN 47403
www.westbowpress.com
1 (866) 928-1240

ISBN: 978-1-4908-5875-3 (sc)
ISBN: 978-1-4908-5876-0 (hc)
ISBN: 978-1-4908-5874-6 (e)

Library of Congress Control Number: 2014919596

Printed in the United States of America.

WestBow Press rev. date: 11/19/2014

This book is dedicated to my family,
who provided me with the best material
a writer could imagine.

Contents

Acknowledgements

Books are not the product of one person alone, and this work is no exception. I'm grateful for many who have assisted me along this journey:

> In particular, I think of my wife, Abigail, and my mother, both of whom labored over the content of my manuscript.
>
> I appreciate those who read and endorsed *Three Ring Circus*—Daniel McCoy, John Price, and Dr. Terese Thonus.
>
> Thanks also to my family, who trusted me with accurately portraying our lives and encouraged me along the way.

Outsiders

I can imagine, mostly from accounts my parents gave, what it was like when they arrived in the Philippines. After disembarking from the plane late at night, they trudged through a room that felt and smelled like a steam cave until they reached customs where they processed my father's passport, then my mother's, and one for each of their three children: Anna, Caleb, and Enoch. Weariness, accompanied by stiff backs and sore muscles, crept through their bodies like old age, to say nothing of sleep deprivation following twenty-six hours of travel. They wandered through the stifling terminal to the baggage claim where they saw a man holding a sign reading, "RBMU," the initials for their mission agency. After introducing themselves, my parents gathered their luggage and headed outside.

Dark-skinned figures were everywhere. Sounds flooded their eardrums: car horns, airport security, and taxi drivers shouting in a language faintly reminiscent of chicken clucks. The humidity wrapped around them, leaving them sweltering and sticky and suffocating, the air almost like water. They stared around like beady-eyed goldfish gulping for air. In the midst of the chaos, they had to wonder: what had they gotten themselves into?

The man from the mission agency herded them through the cacophony and into a van. Once in the vehicle, Dad and Mom could reflect on how they ended up in such strange circumstances. Months before, my parents started investigating mission agencies, including a group called Regions Beyond Missionary Union, and RBMU offered my parents an opportunity to visit a mission site. Dad felt a particular compulsion to work with large communities of people in urban areas who had not heard about Jesus. Though he had an interest in China, the country was no longer open to missionaries. At that time, RBMU was focusing on sending missionaries to the Philippines, and the only urban place in the Philippines that they were targeting was Naga City. RBMU invited my parents to spend five and a half weeks in Naga City in order to get an impression for the environment and ministry.

At the time, my parents' church was not interested in sending them on a short mission trip; few of their staff had gone on such trips. For that matter, the church had never sent a member of their congregation to be a full-time missionary. During that time, Dad, who was the church's evangelism and missions pastor, brought in a renowned speaker named Woody Philips, Sr. to share with the church congregation and mission board. During the question-and-answer time, my father asked Mr. Phillips for his perspective on short-term mission trips.

Mr. Phillips shared how such small visits could save the church money by enabling potential missionaries to experience the foreign environment before making a career move. The standard option at the time was for a missionary to sign up for a four-year term and reevaluate afterward. Most mission agencies estimated that it took the entire first term just to learn the language, adjust to the culture, and start to develop a ministry. If a missionary did not return to the mission field after the first term, all the money that was invested—for a five-person family at that time it was roughly $150,000—would basically go to waste. After seeing the math, the church funded my parents' trip.

Those first five and a half weeks gave my parents a glimpse into missionary life in the Philippines. They were able to live in a house with a national who helped with the chores. My parents attended a local church plant and temporarily led a Bible study. They tasted the foreign cuisine, tried to understand the strange dialect, and toured the city with its congested streets and bright colors. They found it impossible to fully grasp the life they could quickly be living, but the weeks helped them process. Mom had nightmares for the first two weeks after returning stateside, likely because her subconscious was attempting to reconcile the idea of living in the two-thirds world[1] indefinitely. Eventually, though, Dad and Mom decided to join staff with RBMU as missionaries in the Philippines.

It took about a year for my parents to raise all their financial support, and selling their house in Wichita was one of the final elements of transition. Friends and family came over and helped pack my family's belongings and paint the house. My parents decided to sell the house themselves, but it lingered on the market until a week before their departure. Without technological advances like the internet, selling a house in Kansas from the Philippines, even with the help of a realtor, would be problematic. Finally, the house sold, and my family was officially homeless. The last rope on the swinging bridge between the United States and the Philippines had been cut—the ships were burned—there was no turning back.

My parents had adjusted slightly to the Philippines during their prior five-week trip, but culture shock persisted throughout

---

[1] A term used largely by evangelical missionaries to refer to the two-thirds of the world population who live in poverty.

their time there. Indeed, the difference in cultures was so jarring that mission agencies commonly assigned missionaries a month of vacation time every year in order to help diffuse the pressure. Even with special arrangements, many missionaries caved within their first years abroad. They developed health conditions, had mental breakdowns, or simply decided that the stress was too much.

Our later returns to Naga City, via the Pili Airport, included terrifying landings. The runway was, by American standards at least, too short for comfort, with a drop-off at the end. The plane would touch down, the pilot slam on the breaks, and the aircraft shudder to a halt. As the plane turned around at the end of the runway, we could stare down the embankment as the airplane wing hung over empty space. Such a reentry always startled us back into life in the Philippines.

The first challenge my parents and siblings faced was the relentless heat persisting with no end in sight. The temperature, coupled with the humidity, manifested itself in heat rash and listlessness. Air conditioning was rare; a decade passed before my parents rented a house with window units. The rest of the time, everyone relied on fans, assuming the electricity was working. Every room had them—on the ceiling, wall, or propped on the floor—oscillating at full speed. Showers provided another coping mechanism. The water that gushed from the tap was sometimes stained with rust, but it was always frigid. The shocking cold was a veiled blessing that family members sought for relief, temporary though it was, several times throughout the day. We kept a bucket filled with water beside the faucet for the times when there wasn't any water pressure.

However, even the showers had their drawbacks. The bathrooms were a far cry from the typical Western extravagance, with multiple sinks, an enclosed bathtub or shower, and a throne sequestered in its own corner. Lavatories in the Philippines usually afforded a sink, shower, and toilet, but these amenities were often squeezed into a small room with only a curtain shielding the commode from the deluge. On occasion, the toilet was set into the ground, requiring one to squat.

Meanwhile, Mom was particularly disconcerted by the bathroom spectators, as houses throughout the Philippines were populated by small lizards called *butakis*. These tan house geckos were about three inches long, ate insects, and chased each other around light fixtures, besides making Mother uncomfortable when they perched in the corner of bathroom ceilings and stared at her.[2] Though we children would sometimes make lassos out of coconut leaves and use them to catch the house geckos, no amount of population redistribution could relegate the butakis to the outdoors; as the proverb goes, "A lizard can be caught with the hand, yet it is found in kings' palaces" (Proverbs 30:28). Twice Mother was carrying a baby, and a butaki landed on her head as she passed through the doorway. Occasionally, we'd smell something rotten inside the house and find a butaki crushed in a doorjamb. They also left their black-and-white calling card everywhere, particularly on the windowsills, and made it necessary to keep our books pushed all the way back on our shelves lest they lay their white eggs behind the volumes.

Lizard activity even punctuated dinnertime. The butaki has a larger relative called the tokay gecko—or *tokos*, as Filipinos refer to them—that range from eleven to fifteen inches long and are bluish gray in color with orange spots. Though their size kept

---

[2] Mother was also disconcerted by the rats. She once commented that maybe a cat would help with the problem. A local friend, attempting to be helpful, explained, "Well, when the rats are as big as the cats, they don't do you much good."

them semi-outdoors, they took up residence in our ceilings. Rarely seen, they were often heard, their mating calls resounding in the early evening: *to-ko, to-ko, to-ko.* When we did glimpse a tokay gecko, typically all we saw was its triangular head poking out from under the tin roof, the eyes, black slits set in orange irises, watching our every move. As a child, the tokays were a source of fear because they were both fast and aggressive if threatened. A tokay once fell into a tub of rainwater, and when my father tried to kill it with a machete, it latched onto the blade so strongly that my father could bang the knife against the wall without the gecko releasing its grip.

We had other reptilian run-ins. During our first term, my father watched a python emerge from the swamp across from our house and onto the street. As the snake crossed the concrete, it came nose-to-nose with a cat that hissed and spat. While this happened, a cluster of people gathered to watch. Luckily for the cat, the python, which was likely intimidated by the crowd, turned around and slithered back into the grass. Even looped halfway across the road as it was, the snake's head entered the grass before its tail left the cover. The locals later went into the swamp in pursuit of the snake, killed it, and ate it.

When my parents first settled into a house, they diligently hung a thermometer and watched for fluctuations in the climate, which was normal American behavior. Residents of Kansas, where the unofficial motto is "If you don't like the weather, stick around," discuss the weather on every occasion because it always provides something of note. Located east of the Rockies and lacking any significant bodies of water to regulate temperature, the climate swirls with the wind in a cycle of thunderstorms, tornados, drought, sleet, and snow. Boiling summers dash into frigid winters. In Kansas, it's not uncommon for the temperature to fluctuate forty degrees in a day.

The Philippines, however, is about as climatically different from Kansas as possible. Except during hurricanes, the temperature and humidity lingers around the nineties. Dad used to say there were two seasons: hot-wet and hot-dry. Even during the dry season, sweat dripped into damp patches on our clothes that refused to evaporate because the air was already sticky with moisture. At the same time, the country's location along the equator allows for only an hour of fluctuation in sunlight throughout the year.

Until my parents adapted to the setting, they were bewildered when their attempts to use the weather as a topic of small talk were unsuccessful. Normally affable and animated, Filipinos were unresponsive anytime Dad or Mom brought up the weather. The weather didn't change. The locals had to wonder at the purpose of discussing an environmental factor that stayed the same. Why would my parents choose a topic so bland as the weather? One might as well contemplate the lack of speed limits or worry about germs.

Over time, my parents did discover many of the intricacies of acceptable chitchat. Filipinos do make use of social questions like, "How are you?"—a western manner that was likely adopted over the years. Still, the culture retains regional queries, some of which are confusing or intrusive to foreign minds. "Where are you going?" or "Where are you coming from?" seem normal enough, though my mother disliked being asked, "How old are you?" Another common inquiry, "Who are you with?" was more unusual and indicative of social expectations.

To a Filipino, *pakikisama*—togetherness—is a cultural ideal: to be in a group is to be happy; to be alone is a source of great sadness. One's value is contingent on having a place within social groups, like family or friends, coworkers or classmates. This appreciation is peculiar to westerners, who paradoxically idealize extraversion while prizing individuality. In contrast, native Filipinos were baffled when my parents would allow their children to play alone in the house or an infant to cry himself to sleep at nap time; the behavior seemed cruel.

This emphasis on relationships provides much of the rationale behind another unusual question: "Are you married?" Complete strangers, who met seconds before, use this snoopy inquiry as an acceptable part of establishing new friendships. It also comes with appropriate responses. One can answer in the affirmative or is expected to reply, "Not yet." If one simply says, "No," the inquirer will ask for a reason. This question is also directed at children. As a kid, I was always befuddled when Filipinos would ask me if I were married. Wasn't the answer obvious? Yet if I answered in the negative, I would be asked, "Why not?" I was frequently tempted to answer this second question with, "Because I'm eight. And because girls are disgusting."

It was also extremely common, and socially acceptable, to inquire how much one paid for a specific item like a car, a house, or an education. Initially, my parents indignantly assumed this question was part of an attempt to assess how much money they possessed, as they were perceived as rich Americans. Over the years though, they discovered that this behavior was actually a friendly attempt to guarantee that my parents weren't being cheated. If they were overpaying, the local would suggest a different retailer or a reasonable price.

Of course, the new cuisine was an expected area of change. The Filipino diet at its most basic level consists of rice and *ulam*, which is anything that goes with rice. Ulams vary in flavor, and many ulams use meat sparingly, since meat is more expensive than vegetables and fruits. These dishes are prepared along with a wide variety of spices and oriental sauces—fish, oyster, soy—as well as rice wine and vinegar. Coconut juice, fiery peppers, and tiny lime-like fruits called kalamansi are common ingredients. Exotic fruits are plentiful: papaya, pineapple, guava, rambutan, tamarind, and jackfruit, along with a variety of bananas and mangos. Seafood is a frequent part of the diet, and crab, shrimp, squid, and fish take center stage.

Despite the appeal of most of Filipino dishes, there are those that horrify foreigners. *Dinuguan* is pig boiled in its own blood. Likewise, *balut* is boiled duck egg where the embryo is partially developed—different types of balut feature different stages of development, and some even include feathers and a beak. One is expected to crack open the top of the egg, drink the liquid, and then eat the baby duck whole, bones, down, and all. Street sellers will meander around hollering, "Baaaluuut, baaaluuut," which is conceivably a better sales pitch than shouting, "Duck fetuses. Buy your tasty duck fetuses. They're juicy with a slight crunch."

Even *halo-halo*, an iconic dessert that is essentially a frozen shake, features bizarre additions like corn, beans, and purple sweet potato ice cream, and some stores also sell cheese-flavored ice cream. Dogs and cats occupy special places, both in the hearts of their masters and on the dinner table.

Thankfully, Filipino culture provides a convenient way for foreigners to avoid the foods they loathe but are served anyway. Local etiquette revolves around the idea that successful hosting includes an excess of food. Even a routine visit to a friend's house is always accompanied by the host providing *merienda*—a snack and drinks. Unlike Americans, who are not overly concerned if all the meal is eaten, Filipinos are aghast if a festivity runs out of food, implying that the host was too destitute to afford ample provisions. Consequently, people routinely leave food on their plates to signal that they are full, meaning that a foreigner can leave undesirable entrees largely untouched. Eating everything would actually invite another serving—I don't remember Mom ever teaching us children this cultural nuance, likely because it would have given us excuse not to eat okra. In order not to strain their friends, Filipinos will eat part of a meal at home before going to a party so that they will be less of a burden. Furthermore, it is not acceptable to take the last portion of a dish, even if it means going hungry, so that it will appear that the food was sufficient.

Understanding this social expectation would have enabled one of my parents' fellow missionaries to save face. Once, upon being served a meal, this missionary studied the food, quickly lost his appetite, and decided against eating it. When his host stepped out of the room, the missionary spotted an open window nearby. He took his plate and flung the food toward the opening. Only then did he discover that there was a screen on the window. I never heard an account of how he explained the food smashed against the metal mesh and dripping down the wall and onto the floor, but I can imagine his mortification.

Another major amendment in lifestyle was the lack of modern conveniences that Americans take for granted. Dishwashers, dryers, food processors, dehydrators, automobiles, and even refrigerators are amenities that the majority of Filipinos live without. Likewise, many metropolis areas are largely devoid of parking lots. Most of these necessities are met through simple manpower, the cost of labor being cheap enough that most businessmen can afford to hire individuals from the lower class as house helpers and drivers.

For Dad and Mom, this change was a double-edged sword. Inexpensive labor meant my parents were freed from tedious piles of dishes and laundry, spared the process of shopping at the market, where they would have been ripped off anyway, and rescued from the quest for an open parking spot, which meant more time to pursue ministry. Still this task force held decidedly non-western mindsets.

In a culture where time is fluid, punctuality is absent. This meant *katulongs*—house helpers—would show up late for work or not at all, yet they would expect that their absence would not jeopardize their employment. For this reason, many local stores hired twice as many employees in hopes that someone would always show up to work. Meanwhile, every little aspect of the katulongs's work seemed to be diametrically opposed to American sensibility: laundry was allowed to wrinkle and burned with irons while knives had to be kept dull—the novelty of sharp knives provided a constant hazard—and other kitchen utensils were abused as outdoor tools. Often enough, it seemed that Mom would finally finish training a katulong only to have her move, conceive, or in one extreme case die (one of our house helpers miscarried and died from an infection).

Though my family employed katulongs early on, it was years before we hired a driver simply because we could not afford the cost of a vehicle. Not having a car meant my family suddenly had to rely on a foreign transportation system, which was another point of amendment in my parents' previously Midwestern life. Especially considering the crowded population and narrow roads, the Filipino transportation system effectively facilitates city life through the use of two types of motor vehicles—the tricycle and jeepney—though the transportation system is augmented in major cities by the addition of taxis, buses, and trains. The tricycle and jeepney exist in a symbiotic relationship where tricycles run brief freelance errands and jeepneys adhere to dedicated routes throughout the city, between towns, and into the countryside.

The tricycle is a motorcycle with a sidecar that is almost entirely encased by metal, to ward off the sun and rain. While the tricycle will never win an award for speed, appearance, or comfort, it is surprisingly easy to maneuver. The brilliance of the vehicle is that it can easily seat seven people—two behind the driver and four inside the sidecar—for the low fuel cost of operating a motorcycle. Additional luggage can be strapped on top or placed on the rack behind the sidecar. Of course, the idea of seatbelts in such a setting is laughable; like kickstands on racing bicycles, they would just add extra weight and get in the way.

My family was once visited by a tall American weightlifter. The first time he rode a tricycle, my sister Anna instructed him to get on in back, meaning behind the driver. However, the driver and occupants of the tricycle were terrified when the vehicle suddenly reared up on its back wheels. The man had taken a seat on the luggage rack.

The jeepney, the pinnacle of Filipino transportation culture, is essentially an elongated jeep with a bench seat upfront and two long benches facing each other following the length of the vehicle, each propped against the sides walls. This vehicle is the packhorse of transportation. At least three people can squeeze in to the driver's right and one on the left, each of the two rows can seat twelve people, and another five people can stand on the railing along the caboose and hold tight. There are also racks on top, where extra luggage and people can be placed if necessary. People pack in like sardines, shoulder to shoulder, hip to hip, knee to knee. Heat and body odor builds in the packed space where sweat mingles. To say the least, Filipinos have a different understanding of personal body space; to them, the concept doesn't exist.

Each vehicle is decorated with bright colors and hood ornaments and marked with both stations on its route. Jeepneys leave the station when they were full or an egregious amount of time has passed. They pause at special stops along their route and frequently pull over at random to pick up stray passengers if they have extra room, which the drivers perpetually believe they do. Doubtless a map of all the jeepney circuits exists in a transportation headquarters somewhere, but I never saw it. One simply got from place to place by quizzing people about routes and by making many mistakes.

Travelers typically passed payments up to the front, along with a verbal account of the number of passengers the money was compensation for, until it reaches the driver, who counted currency while racing along narrow roads edged by pedestrians. The driver then passed the return change back down the relay system. It was advisable not to sit near the driver if one did not want to spend the duration of the ride passing money back and forth, like a dealer taking bids at a casino. Since payment followed no prescribed order, multiple payments from different locations in the jeepney might transpire concurrently. On more than one occasion, I pocketed the wrong fistful of change, only to have the mistake pointed out by those around me. Still, I was an ignorant American; they all knew mistakes were inevitable.

In order to disembark, we called "*Para*," or rapped our knuckles against the metal roof or banged a coin along the railing. If somehow the signal was missed by the driver, others would take up the word until the repeated call or tapping overcame the din of road and conversation, and the vehicle screeched to a halt. On occasion, a driver might learn your stops, especially if you were Caucasian; whenever the jeepney approached the right corner or house, his eyes in the review mirror would search your own out, and the slightest nod of the head could bring the vehicle to a stop, at which point it was necessary to extricate yourself from the mass of humanity.

You never knew what you might witness on a jeepney. It was not uncommon to see a pig or chickens riding along inside. Indeed cockfighting—a Spanish tradition—provided a sizable gambling industry, and cockfighting rings, though much smaller than football and baseball stadiums, marked the landscape. On a jeepney ride, it was commonplace to sit alongside a rooster, doubtless contemplating its imminent doom or perhaps returning victorious and resting in its proud master's hand, bloodied but alive. In his other hand, the owner might hold the corpse of the deceased fighting cock, part of the victor's spoils, which was long stripped of feathers and entrails but with its head still intact and dripping blood onto the jeepney floor.

The public transportation system was a prime place to discover social protocol. For instance, Filipino drivers consistently honked at the car in front of them before passing, not out of anger but so that the other driver would be aware of the situation. Also, a man was expected to sit with knees apart, yet if a woman sat with her legs spread it implied that she was promiscuous. While Americans spent inane amounts of time and money tanning, Filipinos obsessed over fair skin. They carried umbrellas to shield themselves from the sun, powdered their skin, and bought a variety of products alleged to induce a pale complexion.

This fascination with white skin was paired with an affinity for Western culture, despite how grossly unappealing Hollywood—the Filipino perception of America—truly is. To the nationals, every American man was tall, rich, and handsome, even if he was only five and a half feet tall, wore sackcloth, and sported a unibrow. Consequently, every excursion into the community mirrored the life of a celebrity. People stared and pointed; others hollered, "Joe, Joe," because clearly every white person is named after G.I. Joe. Children, or even adults, touched our arms and legs in passing, to ascertain if our skin was somehow different from their own, not just in appearance but also in texture.

Perhaps best of all, locals assumed that obviously the foreigner doesn't understand *Tagalog* (the national language), and they communally critiqued manners, dress, and other features. When Anna did most of our family's grocery shopping as a teenager, she consistently elicited appraisals when she traveled to the market.

People would comment about her looks or height, and models or actresses they thought she resembled; guys would elbow each other and whisper, "I think she likes you." One of our katulongs, Ate Larry, usually filled the role as Anna's *kasama* (companion), and these whispered critiques made Larry extremely uncomfortable because she knew that Anna understood what was being said. Finally, Ate Larry took to warning the locals beforehand that Anna had an excellent comprehension of the local dialect—the dumb Americans were finally learning.

Reflections of a Reprobate

Like most large families, mine functioned a little differently. My eight siblings and I routinely went through roll call during road trips, answered to whistles, and showered on a schedule. Chores were a necessity, and we lived in hand-me-downs. Perhaps most notably, the older children cared for the younger children. Anna, the eldest, looked out for Esther (child number 5). The second born, Caleb, cared for Abigail (number 8). Enoch, the third oldest, tended to Nathan (number 6), I cared for Josiah (number 7), and Mom looked after baby Hosanna—though these pairings did switch over the years as children aged.

In a family with nine kids, discipline isn't optional—it's mandatory. With Anna, Caleb, Enoch, Luke, Esther, Nathan, Josiah, Abigail, and Hosanna all growing up in one house, rules were sometimes all that separated order from chaos. Especially growing up in the Philippines, commands and punishments kept us safe. Once when Nathan disobeyed, he was bitten in the back of the head by a dog, and on another occasion, I broke the rules by wandering outside the gate of our compound with drastic results.

At the time, I was four years old, and our home felt like a prison designed to protect the world from my curiosity. Enoch and I would often perch in the fork of the *kamias* tree inside our walls and gaze over the border of our penitentiary and out across the grounds beyond. As we'd eat the acidic kamias fruit, which grew in clusters like oblong grapes, we imagined the taste of the fruit from the berry tree beyond our walls.

One day our opportunity to find out how the berries tasted presented itself. Our warden parents were away, our caretaker distracted, and the gate was unlocked. Eager escapees, we seized the chance. To a child, the field beside our house was a Neverland filled with vines, flowers, and adventure. When we arrived at the berry tree, Enoch swiftly ventured into its heights. As I watched his ascent, I stepped back, and the sky and vegetation around me vanished.

Cool liquid grabbed me. The world was suddenly dark and filled with bubbles churning in water. My lungs begged for air. I tried to scream, but the sounds were shoved back down my throat. I didn't know how to swim. My body descended into the darkness like deadweight, despite all my struggling. Then there was something solid underfoot. I kicked off and pushed myself upward.

I broke the surface, finding light again. An earthen circle above and around me hedged me in, framing the pale sky. I could see now the vines that had hidden the well from my sight. Roots hung down toward the water like snakes, just out of my reach. I yelled as I paddled frantically to stay afloat.

Enoch's frightened face peered overhead looking down at me; his features seemed closer to the clouds than to me. He stretched out a stick, I grabbed onto it, and he pulled me upward. He was not strong enough to drag me all the way out, so I grabbed onto the roots and dangled there, still half-immersed, while he scampered away. Long minutes later, Enoch returned with Caleb, who lifted me from the depths. Wet and shaking, I followed them back to the home that suddenly seemed more like a sanctuary than a prison. With such unknown dangers lingering everywhere, rules and discipline were vital, potentially the only barrier between life and death.

As a child, "applying the rod of knowledge to the seat of instruction," as my parents said, was the simplest form of punishment. The idea came from verses like Proverbs 22:15, "Folly is bound up in the heart of a child, but the rod of discipline will drive it far away." The rod, of course, was not technically a rod. Instead, it went through a progression of forms, the most iconic being the spoon, which was really a giant, yellow spork that my mother discovered better served for bottoms than spaghetti noodles. It generally addressed minor offenses, and each misdeed was associated with a specific number of swats. Causing troubles, the most basic offense, warranted only one swat, but other crimes—bank robbery and such—were associated with incrementally larger spankings. Some of us, myself included, avoided spankings while others seemed to have an affinity for them. My punishments never graduated past the basic offenses, but a couple of my brothers eagerly ran the gauntlet. It wasn't that I was a saint; I simply only got caught committing the basic offenses.

Some of my siblings took a little while to fully understand the role of punishment and how they were to respond. As a young child, when Josiah would misbehave, Mom would warn him, "Don't do that. Do you want a spanking?"

He would somberly answer, "Yes," while doing his best to restrain tears.

Likewise, Enoch, almost a decade before, was an extremely stubborn child, and no amount of punishment could keep him in his crib at night. Regardless of how many pats he'd already received, Enoch would climb out of bed, crying the whole time because he knew the consequences of his actions but didn't want to sleep. Finally, Mother discovered that the only way to insure that he stayed in bed was to sit in the doorway of his bedroom so that he realized there was no chance of escape.

On a different occasion, Mother attempted to cure some of the little kids of their practice of biting. Exasperated, she threatened that if anyone showed up with bite marks from a sibling, she would bite the offender as punishment. In order to test this theory, Abigail went to Hosanna and asked her, "Would you please bite me?" Hosanna was confused by the request, but her sister was insistent. Ever the dutiful sister, Hosanna acquiesced. However, no sooner had she complied than Abigail marched to Mom, displayed her arm, and exclaimed, "Hosanna bit me."

Before Mom discovered the spork, she was always searching for the next tool of discipline. When they were kids, Anna and Caleb would scour the house for whatever could possibly be conceived as the next paddle. Then they would extensively test each potential paddle on each other to discern its sensational merit. Any item that stung disappeared. One that did not hurt would be left around for Mother to discover, and when she used that paddle, Anna and Caleb would fake tears (Crying before, after, and during spankings took practice. Not crying meant that the discipline was not severe enough, but excessive crying betrayed a lack of dignity). At one point, Anna and Caleb tricked Mom into using a painless paddle for weeks. It was not until she discovered them secretly laughing that she realized the deception.

It was possibly due to this occurrence that Mother finally settled on the spork as her implement of choice, bought multiple copies, and labeled them—"master bedroom," "living room," and so on. Spork pilfering became a revered art form, and some of my siblings attempted to collect the whole set. Caleb and Nathan in particular took to this sport with the daring of Sir Percy Blakeney, but then I suppose it was Dad and Mom's fault since *The Scarlet*

Pimpernel was on our shelf. An entire stash of stolen spoons was once discovered under Caleb's bed during one family move, and they were quickly repossessed. Afterward, to prevent such a possibility, Nathan began snapping the heads off the sporks he filched.[3]

Though spanking was the simplest form of discipline, it wasn't the primary method. Punishment existed in a variety of forms. Time in the corner was one method: the offender was instructed to sit facing a corner for a specific amount of time—typically five or ten minutes—where he was expected to meditate on his offense. Afterward, the child would make his apology. Other times when conflicts arose between siblings, the two would be sent to different locations of the house. For instance, when Anna and Caleb were young, they would inevitably fight with each other, at which point Anna would be instructed to remain inside while Caleb was sent to the outdoors. Because they were playmates, the two found this punishment especially poignant and would often meet at a window to make up and continue their friendship through the screen. Many years later, a different structure for this penalty was created. The offenders were instructed to sit on the piano bench where they were to remain until they resolved the conflict (though this did nothing to increase our affinity for the musical instrument). Then the parties would share their resolution with the parent who had assigned the penalty.

---

[3] On a side note, I am growing increasingly convinced that American schools should create a new profession, that of a spanker, in order to keep students courteous. The position could be filled by an independent contractor who would be unaffected by the emotions and terms of the offense, and who would circulate from school to school dispensing reparation. When he isn't wielding the yellow spork of justice, he could roam the halls in the garb of the grim reaper or Lucifer or the energizer bunny or really whatever it is kids are afraid of nowadays.

Other times, children were assigned to make so many circuits by walking or running around the house, calling out their current number after each circle or ringing the doorbell, if we were living stateside. The practice provided a healthy punishment while burning off any pent up energy. Once, we had a carpenter working on the house, and he heard the doorbell ring at intervals. After a while he thought, "Doesn't anyone ever answer the door around here?"

Foot rubs were another point of punishment. Mom enjoyed having her feet massaged, so sometimes disobedient children were required to rub her feet for five minutes. Like any form of discipline, my siblings quickly decided that they did not relish the task. Once, after being sentenced, Josiah somberly marched out of the room and returned a few minutes later dressed in scrubs, latex gloves, and a surgical mask, much to everyone's amusement.

Grounding offered a viable option for the older kids—every teenager cherishes his freedom and will negotiate to protect it—although it had its limitations. Once house arrest commenced, other forms of discipline were inconsequential, the worst punishment already being in operation. All our parents could do upon further offense was extend the duration of the grounding, although doing so risked exasperating the child, a possibility my parents were wary of given Paul's warning in Ephesians 6:4. Consequently, grounding existed as a safeguard utilized when other forms of discipline failed.

My parents stopped spankings long before their child entered the teen years, and at some point, they happened upon a unique disciplinary method: reports—extracurricular essays designed to stimulate both morality and intelligence. For example, punching my brother back could result in an essay on aggressive behavior or retaliation, the page length determined by the scale of violence and quantity of blood. Punching somebody once might warrant a three-page paper, but punching someone thrice would triple the length. Therefore punching softly was inadvisable because you would be making poor use of your page count.

The introduction was to include an account of the crime, and many of us became masters of embellishment, recounting the minutest details of the offense, such as time, temperature, and humidity with Tolkienian flair. The body of the work generally pertained to the topic of offense and its converse trait. For example, a report on disrespect could examine both facets of the issue—respect and disrespect—and analyze Biblical stories pertaining to the topic.

The conclusion was expected to include an apology to the affronted as well as the younger siblings, for whom a negative example had been set. It was quite beneficial to have younger siblings to set a bad example for because they filled extra space in a report. For instance, I could apologize to Esther and Nathan and Josiah and Abigail and Hosanna for setting a bad example. Hosanna, on the other hand, was deprived of this loophole. Eventually the younger siblings addressed this discrepancy by insisting that they too could set a bad example for their elder siblings, thus adding to their word count.

The worst part of a report came after the essay was complete. On the due date, the reprobate would present his work to the family at dinner time, much as a doctoral candidate defends his dissertation. The family would critique the assignment, the quality of the word choice, the power of the childish metaphors, sharing both what was liked and what could be improved (It should be mentioned that the practice of writing reports offered an academic advantage to my siblings when we entered public school. Apparently, it occasionally pays to be bad). Finally, the visual form of the essay would be perused to ensure that the writer had fit enough words onto the page. This was necessary because reports could be typed or written by hand, and it was widely known that writing by hand allowed for a smaller word count, as misspelled words or miswritten phrases could be struck through and the spacing between words exaggerated. Consequently, it was necessary for Dad and Mom to insure that this advantage had not been abused overmuch.

After accepting a report, the presiding parent would oversee the essay's destruction, to prevent plagiarism naturally. It is worth noting that the occasional sarcastic flavor of an essay gave cause for subsequent reports on respect. Other times, a parent's mental lapses would save us from having to submit an assignment at all, even if it was already complete. In that case, it was possible to save the report for later use, as a kind of Get Out of Jail Free card. Surprisingly though, a black market for reports was never fully established.

Sometimes, when we kids didn't think the discipline dispensed was adequate for a sibling's offense against us, we took justice into our own hands. At one point, Nathan had a habit of mouthing off whenever the older kids gave him directions, so we complained to Dad and Mom. When they ignored our petition, Enoch and I took action. We first challenged Nathan that if we tied him up, he wouldn't be able to escape. True to form, he dared us to try. Accordingly, we got out the duct tape, tied him hand and foot, and deposited him in our dark basement for a few hours. The beauty of the punishment was that we did not get in trouble because there was nothing malicious about our actions. We were simply helping Nathan test out his theory.

At other times, parental discipline was rendered completely unnecessary as justice seemed to be divinely distributed. It was not unheard of for the kids to exchange blows, and there was an occasion when Caleb and Enoch got into a scuffle that ended with Caleb biting Enoch on the arm. However, instead of being greeted with tears, the aggression elicited gleeful laughter from Enoch that continued for several minutes, to Caleb's utter bewilderment. Finally, he demanded an explanation. Enoch eventually composed himself long enough to share. He had ringworm on his arm, and Caleb's teeth marks encircled the fungal growth perfectly, meaning Caleb had exposed his entire mouth to infection. Caleb was aghast. He dashed to the bathroom where he spent the next half hour frantically sterilizing his mouth with every conceivable disinfectant.

The vast majority of discipline, at least so it seemed, was meted out after school had ended and before dinner concluded, a magical period of the day that we affectionately called the "hour of the valley of the shadow of death" (a term derived from the 23rd Psalm). Mom would be worn out, the kids would be bored or hungry, and both parties were trapped indoors because darkness was setting in. Under such circumstances, even amiable children and saintly parents test the ties of familial affection. Eventually Enoch developed a signal to warn people away from Mother when she was frazzled. After leaving one confrontation, he looked at the siblings, tucked his head into his shirt, and waved his hands over his seemingly absent head. Then he growled, "That means, 'Don't go in there; she'll bite your head off.'" Years later, waving your hands over your ducked head was still a universal warning.

Of course, our parents' attempts to instill a sense of morality in each of us were rarely embraced wholeheartedly. When Mom used to recognize that we were inclining towards sinful behavior, she would caution us by saying, "Sin is knocking at the door." I'm sure her intentions were pure, but this warning rarely did anything but highlight our frustration. One day after hearing this phrase, I went to Anna and parroted, "Be careful. Sin is knocking." Then I hissed, "Come in. Come in. Hurry!"

As people are prone to do, my siblings and I often became experts at following the letter of the law though ignoring its spirit entirely. Once while the parental units were away on a date, we were left with instructions to listen to a Bible tape during lunchtime. We complacently placed the Bible tape in a cassette player and ran it as we ate, but we kept the volume low. Meanwhile, in a different audio device, we played a radio broadcast just loud enough to drown out the Bible reading. When Dad and Mom asked, we assured them that we had played the Bible cassette; technically, that was the truth.

As in all advanced governing systems, it was necessary to find a way to relay new edicts to the whole family, so that no delinquent could claim ignorance. Thus, the family meeting came into existence. This activity occurred every Saturday morning, and like Congress, frequently included lengthy amendments and extensive filibustering that would extend for long enough that we embraced ridiculous policies simply so we could adjourn. Besides, the kids could only ratify laws, not veto them. For example, there were rules pertaining to when one was supposed to go to bed and rise in the morning. Each child's bedtimes hinged on age—the older the child, the later the bedtime. However, everyone was expected to get out of bed at the same time, typically six in the morning, since public school and life in general in the Republic of the Philippines started at seven. No amount of petitioning could change the times; like the Code of Hammurabi, they were written in stone.

These meetings naturally spawned impromptu meetings among the kids, assemblies that I liken to the conventions of our American founding fathers who deliberated on the tyrannical state in which they found themselves. We discussed the latest edicts, their implications for our way of life, and how we would respond. If we presented a united front in opposing a new rule, it might be possible to alter said rule based on a process of appeals to whichever parent we deemed more amicable to our cause. If negotiations failed, civil disobedience was an option. After one such conference, several of my siblings approached Dad and Mom with a list of grievances, such as our parents' policy of scanning our emails. Our attempt failed miserably. Accordingly, many of us turned to different forms of resistance: Enoch and I created our own email addresses, and Esther began writing her letters in white font.

In the end though, it is worth highlighting that these policies and disciplinary practices, objectionable as they were at the time, did pay off. None of my siblings died, and none of us entered adulthood missing limbs or with extensive criminal records. Nowadays, we're all healthy members of society. Of those of us with careers, we have a full-time mom, an engineer, a pastor, a banker, and a medic, not to mention me—though exactly what I am remains to be seen.

Behind Barbwire

One year when my family was returning to Wichita, Kansas from the Philippines, we were on our fourth and final flight, which meant boredom had settled in long ago. Hence the wager: It'd been four years since my family was in America, and in that time, Enoch morphed from a short, chunky kid to a tall, skinny adult with peroxide-bleached hair. The point of controversy was whether or not Enoch could disembark before the other family members and meander right past the crowd of family and friends awaiting our arrival without being recognized.

My father was in the thick of the debate and arranged for Enoch to exit the plane with a few strangers, who happened to be Enoch's age. When our plane nosed into the terminal, the rest of my family waited while Enoch exited the plane. He wandered right past the welcoming committee without raising any suspicions; his own grandmother even noticed him but assumed he was part of a rock band.

When the rest of my family exited the plane, we were greeted with concern and relief. In the midst of the pother, we learned that a missionary couple in the Philippines had been kidnapped by a terrorist organization. No one knew who the missionaries were. As we delayed getting off the plane, members of our welcome party had grown increasingly anxious.

It was 2001. Before long, news stations reported that the couple was named Martin and Gracia Burnham. They were celebrating their anniversary at a resort when armed men arrived by boat and abducted the Burnhams and several other guests. These men were part of a Muslim Terrorist organization called the Abu Sayyaf, which was primarily active in the southern Philippine islands. In addition to being missionaries, like my parents, the hostage couple was also from Rose Hill, Kansas, just a short drive from Wichita; Dad even knew of the Burnhams, though he had never met them.

Over the next year, my family listened and watched. Filipino troops searched for the Abu Sayyaf, but the kidnappers hid in the jungles where they demanded ransom and decapitated some of the hostages. To no avail, U.S. politicians negotiated with Filipino officials in hope of obtaining permission to send in American Special forces; the Filipino government insisted that they would remedy the situation. This was likely an attempt at saving face and a consequence of Filipino history since the Filipino people spent centuries under either Spanish or American rule.

Then Filipino troops surprised the Abu Sayyaf and their three remaining prisoners during an afternoon siesta. The raid was a disaster; the soldiers shot all three of the remaining prisoners, wounding Gracia and killing Martin and the third hostage. Gracia was flown to Kansas where she was reunited with her children and began her recovery. Martin's funeral, a week later, attracted thousands of sympathizers, including my family.

After the Burnham tragedy, people would ask if it was safe for my family to live in the Philippines. Aside from the environmental dangers—hurricanes, earthquakes, and volcanoes—there was the risk of diseases like malaria or rabies. In the American mind, however, the greatest threat was the people. To an extent, this fear was valid. While Filipinos are friendly people, much more so than their western counterparts, they still live in a two-thirds world country. Economic need can fuel desperate actions.

Kidnapping was the obvious fear for missionaries when I was growing up because Caucasians in the Philippines are associated with wealth; every good Filipino knows there are no poor white people, at least not in the Philippines. In order to deter kidnappers, the agency my parents worked with required their missionaries to sign an agreement promising that they would not pay ransom in the event of a kidnapping. Otherwise kidnappers might start targeting missionaries. My siblings and I grew up with an understanding of this policy as my parents explained it to all of us children. Incidentally though, Chinese Filipinos were more likely targets for kidnapping than missionaries because Chinese businessmen were wealthier and considered more likely to pay.

The Abu Sayyaf was not the only terrorist organization active in the Philippines, and kidnappings and bombings were frequent features in the news. The New People's Army—the extremist communist movement—was another fanatic group active throughout our time abroad. Like other violent dissenting parties in the Philippines, the New People's Army is in many ways a vestige of colonialism. When the Spanish conquered the Philippines, many nationals formed parties of resistance who led rebellions throughout the Spanish occupation. Fighting for freedom was a way of life and an occupation for many Filipinos.

When the United States acquired the Philippines along with several other territories during the Spanish-American War, this professional insurrection did not disappear; instead, it shifted focus. Americans became the dictators. These tensions existed throughout the U.S. administration of the Philippines and extended through the Japanese invasion during World War II when Americans and Filipinos formed bonds of brotherhood as they defended the islands. Afterward, the U.S. granted the Philippines its independence.

Even with Filipinos in charge of the country, the families who fought the existing government for generations did not all disperse and adopt new vocations. They regrouped under new causes, whether Communism or Islam, and renewed their resistance. My family's years in the Philippines extended through several coup d'états, including one that was successful and lead to new government leadership.

One of my father's first Filipino disciples was a young amputee by the name of Roy.[4] Every week he visited our house, ate lunch with our family, and spent what seemed like hours praying with my father. Years before, Roy was mentored by a communist professor at the University of the Philippines, in Manila, and he fell in with the New People's Army. One day, he was with a group of N.P.A. members when a fight broke out, and one of Roy's colleagues was killed. Roy went back to the group vehicle, retrieved his pistol, and began taking out the opposition. This was the beginning of Roy's career as a hit-man, a career that snowballed until the government put a price on Roy's head, and the N.P.A. sent Roy to live in the country, near Mount Isarog.

One day, the Filipino army surrounded Roy's house and opened fire. One of Roy's cousins was killed in the exchange, and Roy was shot in the right arm. When he was taken into surgery, instead of repairing the damage to his arm, the doctors amputated it, affectively terminating Roy's career. Then he was sentenced to prison where he met a missionary woman who told him about Jesus.

---

[4] Some of the names in this work have been changed to preserve the privacy of those involved.

There was another man who my father worked with who had an attitude, issues with authority, and a history with the N.P.A. One day, he suddenly disappeared. Nobody knew what happened, though it was suspected that he was shot in the neck and buried—the N.P.A.'s trademark. He left a young wife and baby.

Most of the danger from groups like the Abu Sayyaf or New People's Army could be sidestepped by avoiding the specific areas of the country where they were active. For instance, the Muslim Terrorists stayed predominately in the Southern islands, and the N.P.A. was active in the rural areas of Luzon Island near Mount Isarog. This mountain was not far from where my family lived, and my parents were cautioned to avoid any association with the Filipino or U.S. military.

This same principle of avoiding troubled areas was imperative regarding danger in general. For example, *Centro* constituted the middle of Naga City—the city where we lived for most of our time in the Philippines—and was safe during the day, but at night you ran a higher risk of encountering thugs and the like. One of our Filipino friends was stabbed late at night by members of a street gang, though he recovered. Being safe was often as simple as being in the right place at an appropriate time and taking proper precautions.

Many of the local businesses took extra safety measures as well. One would expect a foreign bank to need security guards as a precaution; however, even many local Filipino fast food chains—like Jollibee or Graceland's—felt the need for extra safety and employed a security guard or two at the front. If the guards ever took a gun safety course, though, it didn't do any good; their sawed-off shotguns were just as often leveled at customers as pointed at the ground or sky.

During our first few years in the Philippines, one of my mother's missionary friends was stabbed in her own home by a burglar. Though she was rushed to a hospital in plenty of time, the hospital staff, not realizing that she had Rh- blood, gave her the wrong kind of transfusion—the Rh factor was rare in the Philippines. The woman died, leaving a husband and three children. Another missionary woman, who had four children, suffered a mental breakdown, most likely because of the vast cultural, social, and environmental differences between the Philippines and the United States. Their family returned to the U.S. within their first term.

Besides these dangers, on an intricate level, the Philippines was, and to my knowledge still is, interlaced with graft and corruption, whether it is a politician selling weapons and ammunition to terrorists or local police turning a blind eye to the sale of illegal fireworks. While countries like the U.S. also deal with corruption, they tend to hide it better. During the beginning of my family's time abroad, a Filipino election was considered relatively peaceful if only thirty to sixty political candidates were assassinated.

Such tensions were bolstered by the way the President and Vice President are chosen. Instead of each Presidential candidate running for election along with their chosen Vice President, each candidate runs alone. The person who receives the most votes becomes President. The runner-up becomes Vice President. This means the President and Vice President hold to conflicting political agendas and had just spent their campaigns gunning for each other.

Government officials lived with armed convoys around them at all times—twice my family went on day outings to another island with a governor who was constantly surrounded by bodyguards. All of this instability fueled corruption on a local level.

For instance, when Enoch went to get his driver's license at the local Land Transportation Office, the government employee administering the test sat down with Enoch and proceeded to fill out the exam saying, "It's okay. I'll take care of it."

After finishing, the man began to grade his own answers and marked a few wrong.

"Why did you mark those answers wrong?" Enoch asked.

The man answered, "If you get everything right, people will think that you cheated."

This same idea applied to academics; a teacher never gave full credit for an assignment because that would suggest dishonesty—a practice my perfectionist sister, Anna, found maddening when she attended a Filipino college.

When you were given a driver's license, it came in a special plastic sleeve, and it was expected that you would keep your identification in the packet and behind it a one hundred peso bill—roughly four dollars. If a cop pulled you over, he would ask for your license, which you would give him in the plastic holder. He would remove the bribe, return the license, and give you a warning.

This practice played an interesting role in the life of one of my parents' friends, Mr. Chan. The day before his wedding, he was pulled over by a cop, and even though he was a Christian, he offered the standard bribe. This particular cop, however, refused the money, confiscating Mr. Chan's license instead. Consequently, the young couple was not able to drive to the hotel where they had reservations for their honeymoon and had to find closer accommodations. As it so happened, the expensive hotel they were originally supposed to honeymoon at was destroyed by an earthquake.

Because the Chan family owned a couple of successful restaurant chains, Mr. Chan's parents' house, or mansion as it seemed to my young mind, had a few safety precautions. One might have assumed their house was designed to protect a family of drug lords. This was close to the truth; the house was previously owned by a gambling ring. The compound was surrounded by a concrete wall at least twelve feet high that was topped with metal spikes, barbwire, and an electrical current. The massive metal gate was secured with steel rods and complete with a guardhouse and intercom system. The home itself had a secret room, and then there were the dogs—German shepherds, Rottweilers, or whatever breed the Chans chose to have at the moment.

My family's first dogs were borrowed from the Chan family, though our safety measures were quite reasonable in comparison. Our fence was only seven or eight feet tall, and while it did have glass and barbwire on top, there was unfortunately no electrical charge. Our gate was made of weaker metal and not very tall, so the motivated were still able to climb over if they chose, though we chained the gates at night to keep anything large from being stolen. An intercom was unnecessary as the house was small enough that a voice could carry across it. We bolted and padlocked all the doors to our house every evening and all the windows had bars, to deter the unsolicited. These measures, though, were not always sufficient.

One of our first guard dogs was a seasoned German shepherd, named Carrots because of the peculiar shape of her nose. Carrots, like most German shepherds, was an excellent family dog, protective yet long suffering when it came to tugging, pulling, or any other annoying childish behavior. On at least one occasion, she observed indulgently as Josiah crawled over to her dog dish, while she was eating, and proceeded to sample the finest of Asian canine cuisine—the leftover chicken bones from one of the Chan's restaurants.

Despite her age, Carrots possessed a fierce loathing for other canines, an attribute we only recognized when Carrot's first act upon arrival was to dispatch our previous dog, a Spitz puppy. The last time the Chans attempted to breed Carrots, she was over ten years old and at least one of her canine teeth had fallen out. Her match was a German shepherd in his prime. Even so, Carrots was less than enthralled with the pairing and made her opinion known by thrashing the stud dog.

Sadly, months after the attempted breeding, Carrots was discovered dead in our yard one morning. My father attributed the death to her age but grew suspicious when our generator was stolen days later, despite being chained to a cast-iron fence. Carrots, Dad realized, had been poisoned. In later housing, my father constructed concrete storage for our generator.

The generator was not the only target of theft. Once Mother woke in the middle of the night, retrieved a glass from the dining room cabinet, and went to tend to the baby—me in this case. The next morning my mother discovered that our van, which was parked in our driveway, had been broken into and the radio partially removed from the dashboard. The attempted theft was likely disturbed by my mother's activity inside the house, only a few dozen feet away; the sound of the cabinet door closing was eerily akin to the click of a break-action shotgun snapping shut. Such fear on the part of the thief was unfounded, though, as at the time foreigners were prohibited from owning firearms.

On a different occasion, mother was sleeping in the master bedroom and awoke to find a coconut branch with a hook tied on the end reaching through the window and into the room, trying to snag her purse. The robber quickly retracted the pole and ran away. Meanwhile our dog at the time, a golden retriever, was penned several yards away but gave no warning, probably in retribution for our caging him.

Aside from having a side mirror randomly stolen, our vehicle was the target of another theft. One evening while in the city of Manila, Father made the mistake of parking our van on the street in a guarded subdivision overnight, instead of inside the fenced compound of the local mission home where we were staying. The following morning, Dad went outside, got into the van, put it in drive, depressed the gas pedal, and heard the axle turning. However, the van didn't budge. When he stepped out, he realized what was wrong. Someone had jacked the vehicle up, placed it upon cinder blocks, and stolen one of the tires.

A couple of our home invasions were done with little subtlety and tact. As attractive young women, my sisters sometimes unintentionally aroused the interest of members of the male population, some who were unsavory, obtuse, or both. On one occasion, a particular suitor waltzed into our house one evening, approached my mother, and said, "Mama, I'm going to marry your daughter." Then he added, "I'm going to go take a shower," and proceeded to the restroom. He was quickly escorted from the premise.

Another intruder, after breaking into our house, announced his presence late at night by turning on the lights as he searched one room of our house and then another. When the activity woke me, I proceeded to load my cap gun and rouse Enoch saying, "Somebody broke in. I'm gonna shoot him." Enoch warned me of the imprudence of such a plan, and instead we woke our teenage brother Caleb, who accosted our guest.

In the midst of the dangers, my parents reminded my siblings and me that our fate ultimately rested in God's hands. Often this didn't mean protection from experiencing danger but protection in the midst of danger.

One day, our house helper, Ning, who was preparing the grill to cook dinner, poured gasoline onto the charcoal and dropped a match into the coal. When the kindling failed to catch flame, Ning poured on more of the liquid. A rogue spark burrowed deep within the coals ignited the stream, transforming the four-liter jug into a flaming Molotov cocktail. Ning attempted to douse the flare with rushed breaths, each mouthful of oxygen only goading the flame on. Caleb rounded the corner, saw Ning, and struck the container out of her hand. The jug fell to the ground, spewing a puddle of flame.

The blaze reared along the side of our house, a billowing, writhing mass of heat that Ning's sister attempted to quench with buckets of water. The flames yawned in response. Carrots, who was still alive at the time, was chained nearby, and Dad rushed to save her from becoming a giant frankfurter. Then he challenged the fiery pylon with an extinguisher, the products of the foam and spray and heat clouding the air. He flung a blanket over the fire, its heavy embrace suffocating the flames. Then shovelfuls of dirt buried the danger. The last breaths of dying embers, imbedded in burnt cloth and soil, passed away unseen.

In the ensuing silence, someone noticed the sign on the concrete. The blaze coated the pale wall of our house in soot—save for one spot. Above the place where the gasoline container had rested, the clean silhouette of a man was visible, white surrounded by black. The figure was imbedded in what was the heart of the inferno where no man could have been standing. When Mom went to photograph the dungy mural, she found Ning was already cleaning the surface. The image, once clear, was smeared by patterns of light and dark. I was too young to remember the wall with the man in the soot, but my parents assure me that the figure was not that of a human but that of an angel.

In the Beginning

Each year on June 5, one part of the day was, more or less, the same. If my parents hadn't already snuck away to a hotel or resort to celebrate their anniversary, the family gathered around a special dinner. We'd sit in an alternating pattern, each older kid beside a younger sibling—Anna with Esther, Caleb with Abigail, Enoch with Nathan, me with Josiah, and Hosanna with Mom. The meal, something decidedly "American," like lasagna or eggplant parmesan, reflected parental tastes. Somewhere during the meal Mom asked a question she posed every year, "Who knows how your father and I met?"

The younger children tried to remember; the older kids glanced at each other, debating whether or not to give a straight reply.

"Was that before the flood?" Caleb asked, with feigned innocence.

Dad smiled. Some of the kids laughed.

"Ha-ha." Mom said. "We're not that old." Then she waited for a while, until someone provided a serious answer.

"You were both born in Chanute," Esther offered. She was generally more interested than the rest of our siblings in my parents' romance.

Chanute, with a population of roughly ten thousand, is located in southeast Kansas. Everyone knows everybody else, and the motto is practically, "We take pride in minding your business." The town is simple: one main street, one movie theater, a smattering of restaurants. It was a few years after my parents' childhoods before Sam Walton deemed the town worthy of a Wal-Mart.

The local sources of entertainment, such as dragging Main Street or the holiday parades, were quaint but not particularly riveting. Just recently, Josiah described Chanute as being like the Shire: the locals sit around eating and talking, and no one ever goes on any adventures. It was an unlikely place for an exciting tale to start.

After Esther's comment, I chimed in, "Mom wouldn't have dated Dad if she'd known him when he was wild."

"That's true," Dad admitted. "I drank and partied. By the time I went to college, I knew all the cops on a first name basis. I wrecked one of my relative's cars one day when I was out drinking, and another time my father had to come pick me up at the local jail. I don't encourage such behavior," he added, looking at us seriously.

"So why did Mom marry you?" Josiah asked. "Wasn't she a teacher's poodle?"

"Teacher's pet?" Anna corrected.

"Yes. I got along with everybody, I played bugle in marching band, and graduated summa cum laude," Mom said.

"So why did you date Dad?"

"Your father was different when I met him."

"Don't forget that Dad's a lot older than Mom," I said. "Six and a half years older. Dad was out of college when Mom was still in high school."

Dad winked at my mother before confessing, "I was a cradle robber."

"What happened in college then?" Esther wanted to know.

"Well, I'd lived my whole life in Chanute, but then I attended the University of Kansas, after a couple years of junior college. The school population was twice as big as Chanute, and in the midst of all those people, I felt isolated. Most weeks, when Friday classes finished, I'd pack my car, pick up a six-pack, and drive the hundred miles to Chanute."

"So what changed?"

"My cousin, Bill, was one of my closest friends. We hunted and fished together, as our fathers had. Bill started attending the University of Kansas years before I did where a friend invited him to attend some of the meetings for a new Christian organization called Campus Crusade for Christ. After a couple weeks, Bill confessed his sins, accepted Jesus' sacrifice, and turned his life over to God.

"I was pretty skeptical. Nobody knew Bill's mistakes better than I did; we drank together and got into trouble. Whenever Bill would try to tell me about Jesus, I'd remind him about all his sins. One time, we were at a bar when Bill tried to share. I climbed on top of the table and shouted, 'God, if you're real, I dare you to strike me dead.'"

"What happened?" one of the children asked, aghast. Some of us imagined God tipping the table out from under my father.

"Nothing happened. I clambered down from the table, triumphant. But you know what? God got the last laugh. He knew I would spend most of my life telling people about Jesus."

"When did you change your mind then?"

"One day I was with my cousin and some of his Christian friends, and one of them took me through a little pamphlet called The Four Spiritual Laws. At the end, he asked if I wanted to pray to receive Jesus. I couldn't think of a reason to say no that time, so I prayed the prayer.

"Still, I didn't do much of anything about my new faith. After a year, though, I'd grown discontent with my lifestyle of academics and drinking."

"One practically necessitates the other," Caleb said, under his breath.

Dad continued on without hearing, "It became apparent to me that it's possible to say you're a Christian but still be just as miserable as before, if you don't begin changing how you live. So I got involved with Crusade through Bible studies, mentor relationships, and conferences."

"Then you met, Mom?"

"Almost. After I graduated, I moved back to Chanute to work for my father while I tried to figure out what I wanted to do with my life."

"And the ice cream shop? You guys met in an ice cream shop called the Tastee Freez," Esther rushed, hoping to hurry my father on to the mushy stuff.

"Yes," Mom said. "I noticed these two guys who started coming to visit the shop where I worked. I knew they were Christian, which appealed to me because I had just embarked on my own spiritual journey.

"I was raised in the church, but I didn't understand the core of the gospel; my focus was on being a good person, and I succeeded. Everybody knew that I was the kind of daughter any parent desires. On the surface, I was perfect. But I knew I wasn't perfect, particularly when it came to my attitudes. I'd get really angry with people, which made me realize that I was wrong inside.

"Then I went on this retreat where a woman explained how people are saved by grace through faith in Jesus. Salvation wasn't about my goodness but God's."

"And then you met Dad at the Tastee Freez," Esther insisted.

"Yes, these two guys came to the Tastee Freez, and I asked my friend about them. She said that their names were Mark and Bill and that Bill was already married."

"Dad had long hair," I interjected, "and a beard too."

"Dad looked like a hippie," Enoch said.

Esther wanted to know why we didn't have pictures, and Anna explained, "It's so the boys won't have an excuse to follow suit."

Mom picked up again. "One time Grandmother was dropping me off at work and your father was sitting there. I turned to my mother and gushed, 'Look. There's Mark Gray.'

"Grandmother gave me a look that said, 'Oh no. What happened to my sensible daughter?'"

Dad interrupted, "When I asked your mother out, she said, 'Yes.' Before our first date, I cut my hair and shaved off my beard."

"Which is a good thing because my father would not have let me go out with such a wild-looking young man. He already knew your dad's reputation," Mom added. "We dated on and off for a few years but not without incident."

"Your father was going to California for training to join staff with Campus Crusade for Christ and was assigned to minister at a university in Billings, Montana. Right before he left, I built up my courage and asked him whether or not he would write back if I wrote to him. He said he would.

"We didn't have the internet or cell phones, and your dad wrote only a postcard."

"Like most men, Dad had mastered the art of communication," Caleb whispered.

"There was a dream, wasn't there? Grandmother had a dream?" Esther interrupted.

"She did. I was at the junior college campus, where I was taking classes, and called home to tell my mother that I'd be studying late. Grandmother told me, that I should come home for dinner because they were going to have pizza; she knew I liked pizza.

"When I got home, I saw that I had a letter waiting for me on the piano. I picked it up, and Grandmother said, 'Before you open it, I want to tell you something: I had a dream last night that Mark flew into town to visit you and flew back the same day. Knowing that wasn't possible, I realized you would be getting a letter from him.'"

"So were things better then?" Esther wondered.

"For a while," one of the younger children answered, knowingly, "but then things got rocky again."

"It wasn't that I didn't like your mother," Dad explained. "I felt quite strongly that we would end up together, but she still had college left. Her parents wanted her to finish school before she married. I didn't see the point of locking the relationship down real tight just then, which meant I still dated other girls."

"What a romantic," Caleb said.

"Meanwhile, I thought we were practically engaged," Mom continued. "Then one year during Christmas, your father's boss instructed the local Crusade staff to stay close for the holidays because they had a big conference coming up immediately afterward. Dad complied by making plans to spend Christmas with the family of a young lady he knew.

"I think he'd mentioned something about it in a letter, but when your dad told me over the phone, I was cold in my response. Even when he offered to return to Kansas instead, I was upset and told your father, in so many words, that I didn't want to see him again."

"And then she started dating another guy," Enoch injected.

"Be quiet," Esther ordered. "Let her tell the story."

"There was a guy who liked me, who I started to date. Then I realized that when I was with my new boyfriend, he always had to have things his way. At one point, he told me that if we ever broke up, he didn't want to be friends anymore. On a Sunday afternoon not long after that, I just knew our relationship was over, so I broke up with him. At the same time, I thought and maybe even prayed, 'I just want a guy to be my friend. Not a boyfriend, just a friend.'"

Dad started up again, "This whole time, in the midst of all these fluctuations and emotions, I couldn't shake this unquantifiable sense that Sherida and I were supposed to end up together. I stopped praying about whether or not she was the right one. Instead, I started praying for our future children and those children's future spouses, though I didn't exactly pray for nine kids. I prayed for children one through four and anymore that might happen along.

"Anyway, a couple hours after your mother broke up with her new boyfriend, I was raising financial support for my work with Crusade and called your mother's house in order to talk with her father. As the operator attempted to connect me with your grandfather, Sherida answered the phone, but her father wasn't home. Still, realizing Sherida was home, I decided to call back and talk to her."

"I took the call," Mom said, "but I was reserved."

"I couldn't understand it," Dad admitted. "Finally, I said, 'Sherida, as I watched the young people around me, I see all these couples who date but the relationship doesn't work out. Then they never talk to each other again. That's not right. I don't know what God has in mind for our relationship, but I want you to know that whatever happens, I want to be your friend.'"

"Those were exactly the words I needed to hear, and our relationship started up again."

"So you got married?" Esther wanted to know.

"Not quite. There was plenty of time to go still. I graduated from junior college in Chanute and transferred to Oral Roberts

University in Oklahoma while your dad moved to Seattle, Washington. All I wanted was to get married, but the wait gave my parents time to grow comfortable with their daughter marrying a young man with a bad past."

"Even once we were engaged, people still objected."

"At one point, the principal of the Chanute elementary school found out that I was engaged, and he eagerly asked my mother, 'Who is Sherida marrying?' When grandmother told him that I was marrying Mark Gray, the principal's face fell. His wife had taught your dad when he was a child."

"I used to call her 'paddle mad' because she spanked me so much," Dad said.

"And then we got married," Mom added, before Esther could ask again.

"But somebody ran into dad's car the day before the wedding," Enoch reminded them.

"We had to borrow Grandfather and Grandmother Willlis's car for the honeymoon."

"Don't forget, you didn't have money to pay for the honeymoon," I reminded my father.

"Well technically that isn't true," Dad corrected. "I'd been traveling back to Kansas and forgot to make arrangements for my paycheck. I prayed about the need and felt like God said to trust Him."

"What happened?"

"The hour before the ceremony, I was studying all the gifts that had already arrived, in case one of them looked like it might be money. Then I thought that if I hurried, I could still ask someone about borrowing money. Instead, I waited, trusting that God would provide.

"Just before the ceremony, my father pulled me aside and said, 'Son, your mother and I want to give you a thousand dollars for your wedding present.' The amount was more than enough to cover the expenses. With that assurance, I floated into the ceremony, and we said our 'I do's.' We've been married ever since."

He leaned over and kissed Mom on the lips.

The boys erupted in chorus. "Gross. We're going to be sick,"

"Get a room," Enoch added.

Jugglers

Well over a decade into my parents' ministry in the Philippines, I remember my father sharing a dream: He said he found himself standing on the edge of a pool. When he peered into the water, he saw a vast number of people lying at the bottom, drowning. Dad realized with growing horror that he recognized many of the people, some of whom were his own children. He dove into the water, grabbed one person, hauled him out, and raced through CPR. He dashed back to the pool and followed the routine over and over again, the entire time screaming for help at the top of his lungs. Then he woke up in a panic. This is how my father feels about the plight of those who don't know Jesus.

Missionaries are primarily associated with evangelism. Paul is heralded as the archetypical missionary who spent the majority of his time sharing the gospel of Jesus Christ. While the basic tenet and premise of missionary work is evangelism, missionary labor is infinitely more complicated than simply evangelizing, and it encompasses a number of other roles. Coming to the Philippines, my parents couldn't just show up and start wandering around sharing about Jesus, at least not effectively.

First, there was the basic language barrier. Though many Filipinos understand some quantity of English and the country's national language is Tagalog, the islands are home to roughly seventy languages—just traveling farther down the road could significantly alter the local vernacular. Not understanding the language left foreigners at a significant disadvantage that could have serious or comical implications.

There's a story I heard about a young man who came to the Philippines on a missions trip who was a little too eager to flirt with the young Filipinas. He asked a local couple how to say, "What is your name?"

The locals responded that he should say, "*Buntis ka ba*?"

The young man quickly put this phrase to use, but it never elicited a warm response. Rather the question seemed to cause offense. As it turns out, the inquiry, "Buntis ka ba?" doesn't truly mean, "What is your name?" Those three Tagalog words actually translate as, "Are you pregnant?"

My parents started their language training in Batangas City, at a school that was utilized by many mission agencies in the Philippines. The first couple years of the language program were broken into four sections. The first two sections were focused locally. The missionaries spent the morning studying lesson plans, learning vocabulary, and practicing pronunciation. In the afternoon, they ventured into the community and had conversations with the locals, using whatever terms and sentences they had learned earlier in the day. Each language student formed some circuit in the community and wandered from visiting a neighbor to interacting with a store vendor to chatting with someone on the street. Typically, it was the poor locals who had more time to spend in these conversations.

Some days my parents learned as much about the culture as the language. On one occasion, they were out together and talking with the peddler at a local *sari-sari*— a miniature convenience store, often no larger than a booth, carrying soda, cigarettes, chips, candy, and items like laundry detergent. During their conversation, the owner's daughter came into the booth wearing her schools clothes, greeted her mother who was interacting with my parents, stood in the background for a little while, and then said goodbye and left. At that point my mother thought, "Her clothes are different now." While standing in sight of total strangers, the girl had modestly changed her outfit by slipping clothes over or under what she was already wearing. In the same way, it was not uncommon to see a person bathing outside, while fully dressed in loose-fitting clothes.

Dad advanced from section to section faster than my mother because she was spending more time caring for and schooling Anna, Caleb, and Enoch. Still, there were plenty of challenges for my father in studying Tagalog. Because he had hunted extensively without earplugs as a child, he had some hearing damage, which made discerning foreign syllables difficult. Additionally, the Filipino approach to intimate conversation does not involve going off to a quiet area; rather Filipinos will turn on the television or go to a bustling room and talk softly, the clamor around them masking any private details.

Once Dad progressed into the third section of language study, he spent more time in Cuenca, a small town about an hour away from Batangas City that was built near the volcanic Mount Taal. The area had a reputation as a center for *albularyo* (witchdoctor) activity. A local church there, led by an Indonesian named Hanna Handojo, was known for prayer and work with the demon-possessed or those facing some form of spiritual oppression, whether it manifested in physical or mental illness. My family experienced the prayers of the Cuenca church firsthand.

The week that my parents decided to move to the Philippines, Enoch slipped in the bathtub and split his chin open. A doctor stitched up the wound, but over the next couple years Enoch continued to reinjure the area over and over again; he jumped from stairs and ran around with the abandonment of a normal rambunctious boy. After a while, my parents gave up on getting new stitches after each recurrence and started closing the split skin with a butterfly bandage. When Dad and Mom started attending the Cuenca church, they brought Enoch to the elders who prayed that the injuries would stop. Afterward, there were no repeat injuries, and Enoch's chin healed.

Since our family couldn't yet afford a car and the roads were quite rough, Dad bought a Yamaha and joined a local motorcycle club as a way to learn more of the language and build relationships. Every Wednesday, he took either Anna or Caleb with him to Cuenca, returned on Saturday, and went to Cuenca again on Sunday morning with the entire family where we interacted with the church. This pattern continued until my father finished all four sections of language school—meaning he was fluent—and our family moved to Naga City.

Even once my parents arrived in Naga City and started working with an established church there, evangelism didn't suddenly become easy or reminiscent of what most American Christians think about when they hear the term. Instead, my parents needed to learn the culture and how to present the gospel in an effective manner.

In America, the most commonly recognized form of evangelism is what I call "stranger evangelism"—where a Christian interacts with someone he or she does not know and talks about spiritual matters. Back in the 1950's, this form of evangelism was quite effective in the U.S. because many people already understood and accepted the basics principles of Christianity. This method, however, has some major drawbacks, particularly as it relates to cross-cultural evangelism.

According to the basic tenants of Filipino manners, it is crucial to avoid offending others in interpersonal interactions and to allow them to escape discomfort in potentially embarrassing situations. Consequently, it is acceptable to be deceptive if it spares the other person's feelings. As a result, a Filipino might fake a conversion to save a missionary from feeling embarrassed, rendering stranger evangelism largely ineffective.

In the midst of cultural politeness, it was also challenging to talk about Jesus with locals because a typical Filipino looks at an American, assumes that he is Protestant, instantly forms mental barriers, and works to distance himself from any interactions about spiritual matters. Protestants are referred to as "born-agains" and shunned for not accepting a Catholic label. Though converts do not face intense persecution, they do encounter societal pressure from family, friends, and coworkers.

Because of the cultural politeness and religious stigma, the primary evangelistic option left to most missionaries in the Philippines is relational evangelism—where Christians build friendships with non-Christians, and as they experience life together, the nonbeliever has the opportunity to see how much of a difference having a relationship with God makes in the life of the believer. Spiritual conversations occur more naturally, and the existing relationship allows for genuine interaction and honesty. As they live life alongside the local population for years or even decades, many missionaries discover cultural elements that enable the nationals to understand Christianity and view it not as some foreign belief system but as a relationship that transforms lives.

However, breakthroughs rarely happen within a short span of time; it is not unusual for missionaries to labor for years without seeing significant results. The question often becomes whether the missionary will persist long enough in his location for spiritual seeds to germinate. Once a few local lives begin to change, it can be as if once impenetrable soil cracks and roots begin to develop. Still for many missionaries the waiting game, coupled with culture shock and other stresses, proves to be too much.

When my parents arrived in Naga City, the area was reputed as a missionary graveyard because so many missionaries had tried to establish churches only to fail. Most left the region or even the mission organization after only a handful of years. My parents endured. For years, Dad and Mom worked with an established church in Naga City; then they, along with another missionary family, branched off and began a new church. They started with a small Bible study group, new groups formed, and eventually the believers decided to hold a Sunday morning service in one of their homes.

Over the years, my parents have given the account of one man, named Edward, who became involved with the church. Edward had an unusual problem for a Filipino: he couldn't control his temper. Once Edward so strongly berated one of his employees that the employee became enraged and attacked him with a machete, swinging it at Edward's head. Edward deflected the blow with his arm, but the blade did permanent damage to the limb. Even though he was a business owner with some degree of success, people knew to be careful about how they treated Edward. One never knew when he might explode.

No one suffered more from Edward's temper than his wife, Elaine, who was in a Bible study with my mother. When Elaine rededicated her life to Jesus, she decided to love and submit to her abusive husband. A man as controlling as Edward couldn't help but notice the difference. One day he asked her, "How do you get to know God?" Elaine gave him a Four Spiritual Laws booklet she'd been given, and her husband trusted Christ. Edward's question also opened the door for my father to building a relationship with him that aided him in maturing as a young Christian. The change in Edward's life was drastic.

I only met Edward after his transformation started. For me, it is difficult to picture him as a man with an anger problem; the man I came to know was friendly and gentle. Still, other people who had known Edward before his conversion took note. Dad and Mom were once around several Rotarian men at a party when one of them, a former classmate of Edward's, approached my father and asked, "Mark, what did you do to Edward?"

"I didn't do anything to Edward," my father explained. "But let me tell you what changed in his life." Then Dad went on to tell the gospel.

For many Filipinos, even if they were not interested in talking about spiritual matters, they were curious about the foreign Americans. The novelty factor allowed my family to invite people to take part in weekly studies that they might not have otherwise considered attending. My parents led studies about dealing with addictions and also taught Tommy Nelson's video series on the Song of Solomon on multiple occasions. To many Catholics, such invitations weren't threatening because they weren't overtly evangelistic. Everyone had areas of addiction, and the idea of studying the Bible's most sensual book couldn't help but evoke curiosity—not to mention my parents had nine children, so apparently their sex life was decent.

Even as my parents labored to discover how they could effectively minister, there were plenty of little adventures along the way. Shortly after moving to Naga City, Esther, who was only a few years old, was playing in our front yard where there was a tall coconut tree. As she was running around, a coconut fell roughly twenty feet from the top of the tree and shattered a pot resting merely feet from Esther's head. Something similar happened to a neighborhood boy, only he was struck on the head and mentally handicapped for the rest of his life. After that, any time there were coconuts in the tree, my parents had someone come over and knock them all down.

It was also during that time that my parents were awoken late at night by a phone call. My father left the master bedroom to answer the phone, but there was no one on the other end. He went back to bed, only to have the phone ring a little while later. This time, it sounded like there was a fax machine on the other side of the call. My father hung up and returned to bed, leaving the bedroom door open. Not long afterward, he saw light and heard a strange noise coming from the kitchen. He rushed into the room to discover sparks shooting out from behind our refrigerator like it was a flare. After unplugging the faulty appliance, my parents studied the scene. Above the refrigerator there were wood cabinets and above them the wood flooring for the second story where the children slept. If a fire had started, it would have quickly raged out of control.

With their current responsibilities and adjustments, my parents probably didn't spend as much time evangelizing as they would have liked; their role as missionaries left them with a host of other tasks. A church is made up of a multitude of parts, which Paul likened to a body with different features fulfilling various roles. On a basic level, you have a pastor who is in charge of shepherding the rest of the church. He usually ministers in a full-time capacity, and as he guides and councils and teaches, he is accountable to the elders of the church—the elders being the most mature Christian leaders who are elected to leadership by the rest of the church and together make the important decisions. Then there are a bunch of other small positions: the musicians direct the times of worship, the Bible study leaders prepare and guide small group discussions, the youth directors are responsible for teaching the children, someone has to prepare communion and manage the finances, all while the needs of the poor and sick have to be considered. The larger the church grows, the more facets of responsibility develop.

When a church is starting out in a community where there are not already mature Christians, the bulk of the duties fall on the missionaries. There may not be a pastor to preach, and there aren't any elders, just a bunch of baby Christians learning how to be elders. As a result, the missionary has to fulfill these various tasks, while training infantile believers how to meet each different need. Since many of the roles could be done full-time, one role becomes primary and the rest secondary, though still demanding lots of attention, and all of this rests on top of the other challenges a missionary faces, such as staying fully funded and dealing with life in a foreign culture. Sharing about Jesus is what mission work is about, but by necessity, it is one ball in a juggling act.

In the midst of understanding missionary work, it's valuable to know that my parents possessed different attitudes about cross-cultural ministry when they got married. For years before they were married, my father desired to be a missionary, specifically a missionary to China. He'd read about the different eras of Protestant missions, starting with the Morovians who lived communal lifestyles and sent one of every four members of their community as missionaries. Dad studied William Carey, who focused on coastal ministry; Hudson Taylor, who moved inland and emulated the culture he lived in rather than westernizing it; and missionaries like Donald McGavern and Cameron Townsend, who targeted isolated groups of people who had never before heard about Jesus. Dad longed to emulate these men.

Before they were married, Mother indulged my father as he shared his aspiration, but she listened with incredulity: she had no interest in going abroad. It's probably fortunate that Mother didn't voice her reservation because my father likely would not have married her if he had recognized her stance. Dad frequently wrote of his desire in letters and expressed it over the phone, which made Mom nervous.

A few months before their wedding, she sat in a garden and prayed. She told God how she thought she was supposed to marry Mark, but he had this fantasy to be a missionary while she didn't want to leave the country. In the midst of her prayer, Mom felt like God said, "Trust me."

It was after their wedding that Dad realized his young bride had no interest in foreign mission work. He was perplexed: he'd felt God's leading to marry my mother, but now she didn't want to go abroad as a missionary. He felt torn. Still, Dad wasn't going to try and lead his wife where she wouldn't want to follow.

In the meantime, my parents continued to work with Campus Crusade for Christ in California. Anna joined the family, my father took a job as the evangelism and missions pastor at a church in Wichita, and Caleb was born shortly after. My father's work responsibilities included stopping by the homes of those who visited the church and training others how to do the same. He helped choose what missionaries the church supported, preached on occasion, and developed a passion in the congregation for sharing the gospel.

Every year the church held what they called "Missions Emphasis Week" when they would focus on mission work. During one week, Dad brought in a missionary speaker named Don Richardson. Twenty years before, Mr. Richardson took his young wife and their infant son into the jungle of Indonesia where they lived among a headhunter cannibal tribe, called the Sawi.

When Mr. Richardson and his wife came to Wichita, they stayed at my parents' house. This was a strategic move on my father's part, whether he realized it at the time or not, because it enabled Mother to see missionaries up close. Mom had this perspective that missionaries were practically angelic beings that never sinned and radiated this aura of purity that cleansed the surrounding darkness. Before the Richardsons arrived, she made sure the house was pristine, including pulling the furniture out and vacuuming behind it. When Dad asked what she was doing, she responded, "I feel like we're about to be visited by the President of the United States." Mom was so stressed about hosting that she suffered from terrible headaches.

Then the visitors arrived, giving my mother a chance to meet Don and Carol. Don was focused and passionate—sometimes described as living at a level of intensity more appropriate for heaven than earth—but Carol was practical and sensible. Immediately, Mom started to see that these missionaries were merely human. They had weaknesses: they got tired during airplane travel; they ate and slept and lived with all the same basic biological needs. Their success on the mission field wasn't because they were supernatural Christians who didn't make mistakes or feel afraid or wrestle with culture shock. They were simply willing to share the gospel, and God used them in that willingness. After more than one visit and extensive conversations with Carol, Mom thought, "Maybe, just maybe God could use me as a missionary."

Almost thirty years later, when I asked my parents why they decided to become missionaries, they spoke about temptation. They shared how when Adam and Eve were tempted in the Garden of Eden and Jesus was tempted in the wilderness, there were three things working to entice them: the lust of the flesh, the lust of the eyes, and the boastful pride of life. Likewise, 1 John 2:16-17 says, "For everything in the world—the lust of the flesh, the lust of the eyes, and the pride of life—comes not from the Father but from the world. The world and its desires pass away, but whoever does the will of God lives forever."

As a young married couple, when my parents observed various people around them, they saw many Christians whose existence seemed to be about acquiring bigger and newer possessions. Dad and Mom thought, "Do we just want to have a nice house, nice car, nice marriage, nice kids, keep up with the Joneses and have as little pain as possible [not that having any of those things is wrong]? Or is God's best for us not middle-class American life?" Eventually, they decided that they did not want their children to witness their parents meandering through life acquiring stuff; rather they wanted their children to experience genuine and vibrant faith.

Cristo-Pagan

I saw the string of flagellants standing along the highway as my family drove to the beach. My brothers stared; my sisters turned away or closed their eyes. The men were shirtless and wore black cloth masks over their faces. They beat themselves with short whips, each string of the whip ending in little wood or metal bars. The bars clacking together with each stroke followed an offbeat rhythm. Blood trickled from lacerated skin, down glossy backs that gleamed crimson in the sunlight, and stained deep into the flagellants' jeans.

Our van filled with childish questions: What were those men doing? Why were they beating themselves? Were they criminals?

My parents did their best to answer: The Filipinos called it *penitensiya.* They did it because they believed that beating themselves granted extra grace from God. They thought perhaps God would be more inclined to forgive their sins or maybe He would heal one of their loved ones.

Mom asked, "What does the Bible say about how we are saved?"

One of the older siblings answered by quoting Ephesians 2:8-9: "For it is grace you have been saved, through faith—and this is not from yourselves, it is a gift of God—not by works, so that no one can boast." In my childish mind, the matter was simple then, and the pieces fell together: my parents were missionaries so Filipinos wouldn't have to hurt themselves anymore.

My parents went as Protestant missionaries to the Philippines, a country that is nominally Roman Catholic. For me, even as a teenager, that knowledge conjured up images of the Spanish Inquisition, Jesuits and Huguenots burning each other in the streets, and monarchs changing their country's religion based on inclination. It also raised a question: If my parents weren't simply perpetuating the religious bickering between sects of Christianity that began hundreds of years before, what were they doing?

It was easy at first and then immensely complicated for me to analyze the similarities and differences between Roman Catholicism and Protestantism, similarities and differences that are significant on both counts. Doing so, however, didn't guide me to the purpose for my parents' time in the Philippines. I heard Dad and Mom acknowledge that they believed that some Catholics understood the gospel and were justified before God, just as they admitted that there were many Protestants who were missing salvation. My parents' perspective reflected 1 Corinthians 15:3-5, "For what I received I passed on as of first importance: that Christ died for our sins according the Scriptures, that he was buried, that he was raised on the third day according to the Scriptures, and that he appeared to Cephas, and then to the Twelve." Father also repeated that he was immensely grateful that the Spanish brought Catholicism to the Philippines. The Filipino people were much closer to understanding the gospel as a result, and the presence of Catholicism prevented the spread of Islam in the Islands.

I knew that not all Filipinos were Roman Catholic; there were also minority Muslim, Mormon, and miscellaneous religious groups. Still, my parents weren't working with these Filipinos; they were working with Catholics. There was also a phrase I heard my parents repeat over and over. They described the religious mentality in the Philippines as being, "Animism with a veneer of Catholicism."

For that statement to make sense to me, I had to learn some Filipino history, starting with a Filipino chieftain named Datu Lapu-lapu. I knew about this man because Lapu-lapu's name and face were imprinted on the centavo coin. I collected Filipino coins; they came in a wide variety of colors, shapes, and sizes, and the centavo coin stood out because it was square and felt like it was made of plastic. My local friends told me that the man on the coin was the Filipinos' first national hero.

Lapu-lapu was one of two powerful *datus* (chieftains) in the Philippines when Ferdinand Magellan discovered the Philippines for Spain hundreds of years before. While one datu paid tribute to Magellan, Lapu-lapu led his warriors against the conquistador, and Magellan was killed in the battle. At the end of the story, my friends were sure to inform me with a grin that Lapu-lapu ate Magellan.

Before he died, though, Magellan began passing Roman Catholicism onto the natives, and it wasn't long before Spanish missionaries sailed to the Philippines. Previously, spirituality among the natives consisted of rituals designed to shield the people from evil spirits, and these animistic beliefs did not vanish with the arrival of Catholicism. The old beliefs lingered. Even those who embraced the Spanish religion could not help bringing their own preconceived notions with them, and animistic ideals integrated into Roman Catholic traditions, spawning a Cristo-pagan creed.

I saw this mingling of religious beliefs in a number of Filipinos referred to as albularyos. Every so often, a member of my family would get sick, and a friend would suggest that we call upon an albularyo. In trying to explain to my parents what an albularyo was, the locals usually translated the name to mean "faith healer," but these healers came across more as witchdoctors with a Roman Catholic guise.

An albularyo might take a Bible verse and write it on a paper, sprinkle it with some herbs, and paste it on a pained body part. He might chant incantations in Latin and likely would provide a charm of some kind, perhaps to protect from bullets or poison or disease. While the services of an albularyo are significantly cheaper than those of a doctor, my parents refused their services and were quick to question what percentage of their results were a matter of folk remedies, spirituality, and placebo effect.

Besides flagellation, the Philippines' syncretistic past also manifests in the practice of ritual crucifixion—a medieval custom that is now shunned by the Roman Catholic Church but lingers on in two-thirds world countries. My family likewise watched pilgrims plod barefoot up mountains as they visited the Stations of the Cross during religious holidays like Good Friday. Such customs are meant to procure atonement for sin or grace for others because it's commonly held that Jesus' death paid only ninety-nine percent of the cost of sin. The remaining percent is the believer's responsibility.

This desire to garner divine favor mimics the old Filipino ideals of spirit appeasement through sacrifice, revealing that Spanish religious beliefs were placed atop a spiritual mindset that was not actually displaced. However, the idea that Jesus' death only paid part of the price of sin completely invalidates Christ's sacrifice—once again making good deeds the method of reconciliation with God rather than the byproduct of a grateful and transformed life.

When some of my sisters attended Catholic schools in the Philippines, they noticed another Cristo-pagan concept. Their Filipino Catholic teachers taught that it does not matter what you believe, provided you fervently follow your beliefs. Christianity, Islam, Buddhism, Hinduism, Atheism—it matters only that one is devout; God will understand. Such pluralistic ideas contradict the teachings of the Bible, including Jesus' words about Himself in John 14:6 where He said, "I am the way and the truth and the life. No one comes to the Father except through me."

Maybe the best icon of spirituality in the Philippines is the religious holiday known as the Peñafrancia Fiesta. Almost every September that my family spent abroad, I watched as the area around Naga City prepared for the region's biggest celebration: streamers were tied to electric poles and telephone lines and draped across the roads, hotels prepared suites that were booked long in advance, and restaurants and bars stocked up on provisions, particularly alcohol, in anticipation of the greatest binge of the year.

Many of my friends, if their families could afford it, left to go on vacation, their exodus fueled by a desire to avoid the impending influx in population. The local populace swelled by tens of thousands, flooding homes and spilling into public areas, crazing the transportation systems and markets—since most Filipino families didn't own a refrigerator, the engorged population had to shop daily for perishable goods. Prices skyrocketed as businesses sold out of their wares.

The entire nine-day festival revolves around the moving of Our Lady of Peñafrancia, a wooden statue of the Virgin Mary, from its normal residence in the Basilica Minore to the Metropolitan Cathedral of Saint John the Evangelist. The image, referred to as *Ina* (mother) by the locals, is a replica of the original Our Lady of Peñafrancia that was made in Spain hundreds of years ago. The statue has its own mythology and was stolen and then returned a couple of decades ago. Filipinos would tell me the legend about the statue's construction, describing how a dog was sacrificed so that its blood could be used to paint the statue. The story goes that when the priests threw the animal's body into the river, it came back to life.

On the first day of the celebration, during the Traslacion Procession—the journey from the Basilica—the statue, along with a relic called the *Divino Rostro*, is carted along on the shoulders of barefoot young men as the epicenter of a protracted parade. For the next week, Naga City hosts civic and military parades, fairs, and cultural shows. On the ninth day, the passage back to the Basilica, the Fluvial Procession, incorporates boats that are floated along the Naga River.

"Parade" is perhaps too structured a word to describe such an occurrence; at least to an American, it implies citizens standing respectfully along sidewalks as an orderly progression of floats and dignitaries pass by. The Traslacion and Fluvial Processions are massive bottlenecks, like watching a python swallow a calf. There are two noteworthy floats, those carrying the Divino Rostro and Ina, which are each transported on the backs of locals who may or may not be inebriated.

This collection of men push their burden through the writhing sea of humanity, much of which is attempting to get as close to the virgin mother as possible. At times the scene verges on riotous. People are shoving each other and yelling, music blasts from speakers, and the cacophony hangs in the air like the humidity, the chaos building with each stifling second. Those who are wealthy or influential watch the pandemonium from a distance, atop hotels or local city buildings that loom above the procession.

The barefooted men surrounding the statue also provide a security force: there's a notion that the presence of a woman on the pagoda will cause disaster. Ina herself is placed upon a giant partial sphere that looks like half a disco ball with the flat side resting on the dais. The spherical shape is intentionally designed to make it difficult for people to touch the statue. Much of the time, priests or acolytes ride atop the platform as a last line of defense for the image; each perches precariously beside the partial orb, beating off any contenders with as much saintly dignity as the occasion allows.

Superstition dictates that touching the clothing of Our Lady of Peñafrancia can bestow supernatural power, blessings, or special grace, motivating many to seek personal audience with Ina, despite clerical objections. The ensuing skirmishes resemble matches of King of the Hill, and my father has video footage of a priest being deposed headfirst into the crowd, his robe scrunched to his waist, his underwear subject to public scrutiny. For the victors, assaulting the statue isn't always enough. They might ride along for a period, waving with monarchial dignity, or seize the robes adorning the image—whether out of misplaced hope for healing or due to the value of the interwoven gold—leaving the Virgin Mary, mother of God, nude before the eyes of revelers.

My childhood friends shared how, during the Fluvial Procession in 1972, devotees chanting, """Viva La Virgen," rushed past road blocks and onto the Colgante Bridge, which overlooked the river. Wood and steel quivered briefly under the weight of the crowd that watched the boats pass underneath. Then the structure collapsed. Over a hundred people were killed in the fall—drowned, crushed by debris, or perhaps electrocuted by the decorative lights that fell into the water with the bridge. Hundreds more were injured.

The scene was mayhem. Those injured fought their way out of the water; the crowd on the shore wailed along with police and ambulances sirens. For hours afterward, people waded into the murky water, probing for cold corpses amidst the rubble in order to retrieve the deceased. It was a somber end to the nine days of festivities. The people recounting the event for me ended their recollection with an explanation for the disaster: Ina was angry because the population was not suitably devout. Their fervor was not great enough. She had not been appeased.

Nine, Last I Checked

My parents were married for two years and waiting another year before trying to conceive when they had a birth control malfunction. Weeks later, they knew Mom was pregnant. This sudden deviation from the plan was particularly difficult for my mother. My parents were both on staff with Campus Crusade for Christ, and Mom was passionate about working with college girls. The responsibilities of being a parent threatened that dream. It was only after Anna was born that Mom started to get excited about motherhood—she also discovered that being a mother bolstered her campus ministry as having an infant around made Mom more appealing to female students.

It's easy to assume my parents never used birth control and that they always planned on having nine children. Even as their fourth child, it's easy for me to forget that Dad and Mom's beliefs about reproduction and family planning are the result of a long journey that was both complicated and stressful. It took my parents over a decade to slog to where they stand today, and their position now is a matter of conviction, not a matter of convenience.

A little over a year after Anna's birth, my parents conceived again—this time intentionally. This pregnancy was particularly difficult because the health complications went beyond morning sickness, and my parents worried that they might lose the baby. Still, Caleb was born months later. Three years transpired before my parents tried once more, conceiving Enoch, who joined the family nine months later. Then there was another two-year lull, because of birth control not because of any biological challenges. My father sometimes jokingly referred to my mother as Fertile Myrtle since he could practically glance at her and she would conceive.

This gap in the birth order also coincided with my parents' transition into ministry abroad; it was during these years that my parents investigated mission agencies, visited the Philippines, and raised support. An extra baby would have meant added responsibilities, so they decided to put off reproduction until after their arrival in the Philippines. While Dad originally wanted to have a big family, the responsibilities of having three children sunk in, and when he reflected he thought, "No. Not interested in a big family. You're right, Sherida. Two to four children works great for me."

Around that same point, my parents were questioning how they were going to educate their children in the Philippines. There were limited options available. Sending their kids to a local Filipino school meant risking that their children might not get a western education or be accepted back into the U.S. public school system without major hassles. They could place Anna and Caleb in the missionary boarding school in Manila, but that would've been akin to exiling their kids to an orphanage—albeit one with high education standards.

Later when my family returned for our first home assignment, my parents were extremely dissatisfied with the American school system: there was bullying, peer pressure, and even in middle school, some of Anna's peers were already sexually active. Furthermore, Dad and Mom were forced to tutor Anna through homework in the evening as she wasn't learning her lessons in class.

In the midst of all the questions and frustrations, Dad and Mom decided that home schooling, which was on the rise in the American Midwest, was the best option. As a matter of curiosity, my mother had done her thesis in college on "Christian Education in the Home" without the intention of putting such knowledge into practice. My parents began to investigate potential curriculums and spoke with home schooling families.

It is no secret that home schooling materials tend to promote large families. At one point, my mother was at a Greg Harris Home Schooling conference, and while he was speaking, he went through the materials for sale on the book table. In particular, he emphasized a book entitled *The Way Home: Beyond Feminism and Back to Reality* by Mary Pride. After the session, Mom went by the table, read the back cover, which endorsed not using birth control, and quickly decided that she did not want anything to do with such a book.

In the next month before my parents left for the Philippines, a home school mom randomly came to our house and said, "I know you're thinking of home schooling," and then she highly recommended another book by Mary Pride on home school curriculum. "I know it's expensive," she said, "but I think it would be good for you to buy it." Then she left.

After that recommendation, Mom decided she would order the Mary Pride book on home school curriculum, and while she was at it, she ordered *The Way Home* as well. Little did Mom realize how the book would initiate the major dispute she would have with God in her life. Her original trepidation and reluctance toward mission work was a scuffle by comparison—what was to come practically a brawl.

When my family arrived in the Philippines, Mother started reading *The Way Home*. It was, after all, the shorter of the two books. Mary Pride's book puts forth some pretty radical ideas. She highlights the way that the Bible consistently speaks of children as a blessing—"the heritage of the Lord," as one psalmist wrote. Her writing stresses how the Bible describes God as able to open and close the womb—an ability which people have done their best to wrench from the hands of God through birth control—and claims that birth control perverts the way our bodies are designed to function. Mary Pride also emphasizes that "Family planning is the mother of abortion. A generation had to be indoctrinated in the ideal of planning children around personal convenience before abortion could become popular" (77).[5] Mom hated those lines.

Facing such an extreme perspective forced my mom to struggle anew with questions about the size of our family. Were she and my father in fact limiting God's desire to bless their family and the world around them because of their own selfish desires or because of worries about time and money and other valid concerns? Were her desires more important than God's plan?

This inner conflict built until Mom finally put her struggle to the test. With the move to the Philippines complete, my parents decided to try and conceive again. Unbeknownst to my father though, Mom prayed, in essence, "God, I don't know if all these things Mary Pride is saying are true, but the Bible does talk about You being able to open and close the womb. Mark and I are just about to stop using birth control again. I know I'm Fertile Myrtle. So if we should be leaving our reproductive decisions up to You and not trying to control them, prove it. Keep me from conceiving for the next six months."

As the days slipped by, Mother did not conceive. She found herself thinking, "Huh, I'm not pregnant." Days turned to weeks; weeks turned to a month. Mom thought, "I'm still not pregnant."

---

[5] Pride, Mary. *The Way Home*. Westchester, Illinois: Crossway Books, a division of Good News Publishers, 1985.

My father started to be concerned—his wife still had not told him about her prayer. "She's not pregnant," he wondered. Getting pregnant had always been as simple as falling out of bed. Was he not doing something right? Were babies conceived differently in the Philippines? Months slipped by and no pregnancy. Concern turned to worry, as he thought, "Sherida, you're still not pregnant." Then finally the sixth month passed, and abruptly, supernaturally I like to say, Mother conceived me.

The pregnancy was not an easy one. It was during this time that one of mother's close friends, a fellow missionary lady, was stabbed at home and died, leaving her husband and three children behind. If the loss was not enough, Mom had to deal with the realization that safety was an illusion. Death could come at any time and steal any member of the family; we were vulnerable. The Philippines suddenly seemed a hostile place. In the midst of the loss and the stress, a friend told Mother that it was a wonder that she had not lost the pregnancy.

In tandem, Mother wrestled with the question of family size. She had tested God; she had asked not to conceive for six months, and she hadn't. As she spent part of her pregnancy in bed, she found herself thinking, "Oh my. Oh no. What do I do with this information now?" For nine months she processed and struggled with God.

Eventually Mother told my father about her prayer. She explained her struggle in reading *The Way Home* and how she was wrestling with the implications of the answered prayer. Eventually she told Dad, "For me the answer [about whether or not to use birth control] is no. But you are my husband, I am under your authority, and I will do what you want. So the decision is up to you."

Suddenly my father was under an immense amount of pressure. He certainly didn't want to tell God, "No," so he initially responded, "I guess for now we'll just not use birth control. And we'll see what we decide."

Predictably, Mom conceived for a fifth time. Mom always had difficult pregnancies: Anna was born cesarean, there was hemorrhaging during several of Mother's pregnancies, and she endured months of nausea and appetite loss, often losing weight during her pregnancies. Unlike my maternal grandmother who always felt healthiest when she was pregnant, Mother was frequently ill and miserable for long stretches. This time she lost the pregnancy.

It was during the first trimester and my parents were excited about the new addition when one day Mom started having cramps. She lay down on her bed and eventually miscarried. Our family had a little service where we buried the baby, the older children now approaching their teens wrestling with death, saying goodbye to the sibling they would never meet on earth. Anna remembers being impressed that my parents could experience such loss and sadness without bitterness or anger and that they could still believe God was good in the face of tragedy.

Before the end of my parents' first term, my parents conceived Esther, and she was born during that first home assignment, or furlough. The normal policy was for missionaries to be on the field for four years and then return to their home country for the next year. To those on the outside, this fifth year appeared to be a vacation, although most of the time was spent raising financial support. Home assignments could be more stressful than the years abroad.

The latest addition to our family brought heavy scrutiny as we were now a family of seven. During our furlough, my father was approached by one of the members of the missions board from our largest supporting church who told him, "You know, Mr. Gray, there are those who question whether missionary couples should have as many children as you do." Her message was clear: Five kids were too many; there better not be any more.

This mindset, that missionaries should not have more than a few kids, was extremely prevalent at the time, and to an extent such a mentality is logical. Missionary families have to travel extensively; additional family members mean additional costs and can demand extra attention. The common practice was for missionaries to have one or two or perhaps even three or four children, often conveniently spaced several years apart.

Besides all the social pressure that my parents, particularly my father, were under, each child brought an additional financial burden. Having another child meant raising extra monetary support, a responsibility Dad took seriously. That furlough in particular, there were already some major financial needs—more so than any other furlough our family experienced later on—and having two additional kids increased the amount of money they needed to raise. With the intertwining pressure from the church, the stress of raising support, and the struggle over birth control, tension between my parents ratcheted higher. When they celebrated their anniversary that year, they left for a few days while friends watched the kids. Almost their entire getaway was tense because of the birth control question.

The end of the furlough year came and passed, but my family stayed in Kansas; we did not have enough new financial support to return to the Philippines. Dad considered whether he needed to leave the Wichita area and go off by himself in order to raise funding in other cities, an idea that Mother opposed because she did not want to be separated from her husband. Eventually, my father agreed and continued to focus on raising support in Wichita.

At the same time Mom also encouraged my father to read *The Way Home*, an idea my father was reluctant toward, but marriage necessitates compromises. As Dad read, he was challenged by the ideas Mary Pride puts forth, particularly the line connecting birth control and abortion on demand. Still, my father remained unconvinced.

During this time, the Summer of Mercy took place. This movement started with small gatherings near the three abortion clinics in Wichita where people prayed against the local abortion industry and planned rallies and peaceful protests for the following days. My parents began to get involved, and many of our days and nights were spent with our family attending the protests or holding signs along roads. The size of the gatherings grew rapidly in numbers, the movement capturing national media attention as the amount of people uniting for the rights of the unborn increased. The city of Wichita itself seemed torn over the topic. People everywhere spoke about the activism; in the grocery store the citizenry could be heard alternately praising and condemning the radical activity.

The most extreme aspect of the Summer of Mercy was the "rescues" when people physically, though nonviolently, blocked the entrances to the abortion clinics so that people could not get into the buildings. Men and women would sit on driveways and obstruct the entryways until police came to arrest them. Then the individuals would take baby steps as they walked to the police cruiser, an activity that became known as the "Wichita Walk." One day, pastors from around the city took part in blocking the entryways, and so many men participated that the cops brought in a bus to transport them to the police department.

My father was arrested three times during protests, spending a total of ten days in jail. The first time he was booked and released almost immediately; the second time, his stay was a little longer, and the third time he was in jail for over a week. While Dad was incarcerated, our mission agency called to see how the family was doing. After talking to my mother for a while, they asked if my father was available. She said that he wasn't, and when they asked why, Mom told them, "Well, he's in jail." The mission agency was aware of the Summer of Mercy and had questions and expressed concern, but there was not any kind of reprimand.

The jail where Dad stayed was well furnished, and my father received respectable treatment. Being confined afforded an excess of time for reflection. Those lines from Mary Pride's book circled in his head: "Family planning is the mother of abortion. A generation had to be indoctrinated in the ideal of planning children around personal convenience before abortion could become popular."

Many of Dad's prison mates, some who were devoting their lives to speaking up for the unborn and spending months in prison for their beliefs, were saying similar things. Stripped of his freedom, condemned for his convictions, and isolated from his family, my father decided to reject his own fear about providing for his family, as well as the work and social pressures, and trust God with the size of his family. To this day, my father jokes that Mary Pride got my mother pregnant.

Relinquishing control to God didn't mean everything suddenly got easy. Dad made little progress raising support, and whatever door he tried seemed to be locked. To compound matters, living in the U.S. costs more than living in the Philippines, and the family budget could not maintain the extra expense long term; each additional month in the U.S. drained our financial account. Dad eventually decided, with resignation, that the only option left was to return to the Philippines and raise support from a distance, or we might never be able to return to the field.

At the same time, without the implementation of birth control, Mother conceived again—this time with Nathan. Because of all the pressure from the church and scrutiny from those around our family, my parents decided to keep the pregnancy quiet until they were back in the Philippines. Before our family's departure, several of my parents' friends held a going away party. During the celebration, one of my mother's close friends leaned over and asked, "Are you pregnant?"

"I think so," Mom whispered back, "but don't tell anyone."

The pressure on my parents because of our growing family size continued for several years. Josiah, Abigail, and Hosanna joined the clan, swelling our number to eleven, and each addition brought more scrutiny and more uncouth comments. Even as a child, I was aware that we were under constant inspection. I remember one year when we were visited in the Philippines by the missions pastor of our primary supporting church. He was visiting in order to assess my parents' ministry. I remember as a five or six year old child approaching him and asking, with all my trademark tact and subtleness, "Are you going to stop supporting my family?"

Thankfully, there were individuals who did intercede for my family and defend my parents' decision when others were judgmental. There was a lady named Mary who, when people spoke ill of our family size, would say, "They're raising future leaders."

There was a missions pastor at a different church, named Dr. Dairel O'Bar, who I remember once telling the congregation, "What you see here are not just a couple of missionaries; what you see is a group of missionaries. In supporting them, we are not just sending two missionaries. Rather, we are supporting a family of missionaries." People like Mary and Dr. O'Bar refreshed my parents.

Still there were times of trouble. During my parents' third term in the Philippines, Mom miscarried not once but twice—the last lost pregnancy in particular was life threatening—and my mother ended up in the hospital. The miscarriages brought severe criticism from people in the U.S. Not long after, Mother had some medical concerns that ultimately necessitated a hysterectomy, and the reproductive chapter of my parents' lives slammed shut with a surgeon's scalpel.

It's curious to watch my parents now, over a decade removed from the potential for diapers, with Hosanna a senior in high school. If hindsight is better than foresight as they say, Dad and Mom should see more clearly today than ever before. They haven't recanted; if anything they're more staunch advocates for large families than ever before. All the hard work, the lack of sleep, and the shortage of time hasn't diminished their position.

The Annals of Gray Illnesses

Growing up in a large family meant reliable exposure to sickness of one form or another. With five boys and four girls running around, even mild illnesses tended to resemble plagues as multiple members of the family would contract the illness at the same time. While the diseases and injuries were rarely enjoyable, they did keep life interesting, much in the same way typhoons broke up the monotony of the tropical year in the Philippines. Besides, amongst the kids, bouts with sickness and scars gave one a sense of distinction.

The most heralded virus in Gray lore began with a piece of candy, a piece of candy from strangers no less. These outsiders were local children beyond our fence who happened to have hepatitis. Esther, who was only three, contracted the disease when they generously shared their candy with her. At the time, Esther also had an affinity for the taste of toothpaste, an addiction that she fed by making her toddling rotation around the house, perusing the bathrooms where she sampled each accessible tube, regardless of brand, flavor, color, texture, or expiration date.

Normally, this odd craving was harmless, if rather disgusting, but once Esther was infected, her compulsion provided a medium for the pathogen to spread. Before long, every faithful hygienist in the family joined the club of sallow skin and amber eyes. My parents naturally contracted the severest cases, and eventually Dad was checked into a local hospital. Every other member of the family who was of teeth-brushing age caught a milder case, everyone that is except for Enoch and me. We never got hepatitis; we didn't brush our teeth. This is likely the only story in existence where not brushing one's teeth actually pays off.

I was immensely concerned by my unaltered health and worried that I was going to be punished for not being sick; my wellbeing attested to my disobedience. Should I confess? Or perhaps I should concoct some tale whereby I dutifully risked exposure but escaped unscathed, much like Paul described believers drinking poison or handling serpents, a sign of election and divine favor. Maybe I was healthy simply because God loved me better. Enoch, for his part, indignantly maintains that he kept his own secret stash of toothpaste, though evidence sustaining this claim was never provided. All these worries were needless in the end. My parents, simply grateful that some of the family members escaped, never thought twice about how.

Since sickness usually spread through the family at an accelerated rate, it was typical for an impromptu sick unit to form, normally in close proximity to the bathroom, because, as the saying goes, "Misery loves company." The makeshift hospital became a collection of blankets and pillows where we kids entertained ourselves by analyzing literature, like *Paradise Lost* or *The Wasteland*, and we practiced our bard skills by telling tales from yore—our concept of yore spanning, at most, a decade. The experience resembled a slumber party: we were left to our own devices for the most part, drank Sprite or 7-Up, and watched the occasional movie, all in the unadulterated company of our closest cohorts. While we had crackers and toast rather than pizza and chips, the larger differences were that everyone went to bed early and someone threw up on the hour—on the bright side, Sprite and 7-up taste just as good the second time around.

As time went on, our revelry would increase, the boon of companionship filling us with pleasure greater than the sunshine we never saw. The worse the epidemic was, the longer the festivities extended; it was a wonder we didn't get sick on purpose. When health returned, we were genuinely depressed. During at least one particularly joyous case of the flu, my brothers and I kept a tally of who had puked the most or experienced some other pleasant bodily function. As the number of journeys to the bathroom grew in frequency, the competition grew quite fierce, with wagers being made and prizes assigned for the greatest feats of self-degradation.

It was likely during one such contest that one of my younger brothers pounded at the bathroom entrance while I was inside, hollering that he had to be let in at once. When I opened the door, he pranced in and proceeded to rip off all his clothes—at that age he felt the necessity to remove all encumbrances before utilizing the latrine. Then, stark raving naked, he leapt from his position toward the toilet seat a few feet away, doubtless attempting to match some Olympic record. Much as his acrobatics were to be admired, his timing was imperfect, and he left a delicate russet trail in route to the porcelain throne. Thus the term "toilet jumping" entered the Gray vernacular.

Considering that the Philippine Islands compose a two-thirds world country, it's no surprise that excursions into Filipino hospitals were rarely pleasant which is why my siblings and I were hospitalized only under unyielding circumstances or emergencies. I was born in a Manila hospital within my parents' first years in the Philippines. During her stay, Mom was shocked when her dinner included a bowl of soup with an entire fish head; little did she realize that she had been given what was culturally the prime cut—an opinion with which I actually concur as the most tender and flavorful meat is located on a fish's head.

A few days later, Mother called the nurse into her room and asked, "Could you please dispose of my mouse?"

"We don't have any mice," The nurse answered.

"No. The mouse over there, on the sticky paper." Mother insisted. My father had set up the trap the night before at Mom's request because she'd observed a frequent visitor of the rodent kind.

On that same visit, Mother also discovered that the nurses were often negligent—going to a hospital was sometimes akin to checking into an insane asylum or living in a pet shop. Not only did the nurses insist that I be kept in a special room with dozens of other babies, but when Mom visited she discovered the nurses gabbing away, oblivious to the fact that I was coughing up blood.

Even just before my birth, there were complications. When Mom was in labor, one of the nurses, unaware that my father had been cleared to enter the delivery room—which a husband is not usually allowed to do in the Philippines—insisted that my father stay outside. Dad, who had attended the births of all his children, was unwilling to consent. Still the nurse remained obstinate, physically blocking him from entering the room even though my father loomed above her. Finally, my father, the missionary, politely informed her, "Lady, I have never hit a woman, but I am bigger than you, and I'm coming in." She moved.

After such an experience, it was quite rational that next time Mom was pregnant she opted for a midwifery clinic and later home births. The home births, however, were not without adventure. When Mom went into labor with Abby, my Dad transformed the living room into a theater showing a documentary of the Civil War, in order to keep the kids entertained, while the adjacent master bedroom was transformed into a hospital ward where Mother contended with childbirth. My sister, Anna, who was still a teenager but had some midwifery experience, tried to contact the physician on our unreliable telephone. When her efforts proved futile, my father went to confront the device.

On the march back from placing the call, Dad was distracted by one of the climactic battle's scenes. Transfixed, he stood there in the demilitarized zone between the Civil War and the nearby birthing watching the cannons sound and the casualties mount, oblivious to Mother's calls, which melded with the cries of the dying. Scarcely a few feet away, amidst the shrieks and gore, Mom's labor intensified, right during the heart of the battle of Gettysburg. Where a nurse failed in her fiercest efforts to keep my father from witnessing the birth of his child, a VHS tape almost succeeded.

Eventually however, Dad returned to the bedroom where my mother was on the verge of childbirth. The doctor still had not arrived, so my father rushed to the master bathroom to wash his hands. While he was away, Anna caught Abigail as she was born. The doctor showed up not long after, and it has long been postulated that Anna actually dropped Abigail when she was born, explaining Abby's occasional blond tendencies.

Not all health complications were the result of natural causes like childbirth or diseases; many of them were mishaps of one form or other. Some of them were accidents or the result of carelessness and others the byproduct of sibling rivalry. On a jeepney ride up the side of a volcano, when Caleb grabbed a piece of grass, its fine edge ripped into his finger, requiring stitches. Likewise a duel with plastic baseball bats sent me to the hospital with a hernia; sadly the scar from my hernia surgery, given its location near my appendix, wasn't one I could showcase.

Ultimately some of my siblings' injurious experiences stand above the rest, deserving special recognition. Amongst several of the missionaries in the Philippines, it was common to annually assign an award to those who suffered the worst incident. In the same spirit, I think it reasonable to acknowledge some of my siblings' best efforts in the area of bodily injury.

The award for Most Graceful Injury goes to Esther. As a child, I was once practicing the piano in our living room when Esther began pestering me to play with her. True to form, she was not to be dissuaded and kept pleading for me to join her for a game of Ring Around the Rosy, until I finally complied out of exasperation. Only as we spun round and round, I went so fast that when we fell down, Esther knocked her two front teeth out on the tile floor.

Our first response, quite naturally, was to reinsert her teeth. How were we to know they wouldn't, like plants, simply regrow their roots? Thankfully, Esther's permanent teeth grew in a few years later. In my defense, it is worth mentioning that the loss of her two front teeth did cure Esther of any problems she had with biting others.

Enoch wins the award for Finest Showmanship. As a small child, his attempted career as a stuntman began with him slipping in the bathtub and splitting his chin open. Later, he placed a piece of paper on our tile floor, ascended the nearby stairs, and attempted to leap onto the flimsy target. His aim was perfect, but his understanding of physics was lacking; the glossy sheet shot from under him, landing him on his chin and needing medical attention yet again. Enoch reopened this wound at least seven times.

Still, Enoch's exploits were far from done. As a teenager, he gave a fascinating demonstration, resplendent with gore, to his friends about how to properly utilize a machete. He selected a branch, trimmed it of twigs, placed it upon the ground, prepared to cut it in two, and ended his display by nearly hacking his thumb in half, which required a handful of stitches. Lastly, Enoch's fine antics on a trampoline landed him in the hospital with a broken arm. However, it is only impartial to highlight that this final performance would have never been possible without the assistance of Caleb who gave Enoch momentum in the right trajectory.

Lastly, the award for Best Victim goes to Josiah, though he would never have earned this award without Nathan who doubtless escaped injury only because of his firm belief that it is better to give than to receive. One day, Nathan's argument with Esther about her hairbrush ended with Nathan throwing the hairbrush onto the top of a shelf that stretched all the way to the ceiling. Esther demanded that Nathan retrieve it or she would tell Mom, so Nathan began free climbing the shelf. Josiah, ever the faithful companion, came along to help. They managed to secure the hairbrush, only to discover that they had no idea how to descend. While Nathan panicked, Esther began shouting commands about how to descend. "There's a foot hold under your left foot. Stretch for it. Now let go."

Josiah, not realizing these instructions were meant for Nathan, let go, fell several feet, and split his lip open on the corner of a chair.

Similarly, a few years later, Josiah found himself the victim yet again when he and Nathan got in a scuffle over who was going to sit on one particular chair, though naturally an identical chair was merely a few feet away. Both of them were perched atop the coveted piece of furniture when it toppled over and fell, with the grace of an obese water buffalo, on top of Josiah's foot. The impact shattered his big toe—Josiah's big toe that is, not the water buffalo's—splitting his toenail in the process. Josiah, it would seem, has a rather unfortunate love-hate relationship with chairs: he loves them, and they like to damage his person.

After the injury, Enoch calmly decided that the first course of action was to make sure that the wound did not get infected, so he sat there for the next fifteen minutes squirting hydrogen peroxide onto the injury while Josiah writhed in pain. At some point, I believe this plan stopped being about sanitation and started being about entertainment. Even after surgery and a full recovery, Josiah's toe remained slightly misshapen and the mention of hydrogen peroxide produced great fear and trembling.

For it seems to me that God has put us apostles on display at the end of the procession, like those condemned to die in the arena. We have been made a spectacle to the whole universe, to angels as well as to human beings.
1 Corinthians 4:9

Life in the Circus

When my parents decided to move to the Philippines as missionaries, they started the fundraising process, and not in a one-time sense but in an annual sense; they needed for people and churches to commit to giving monthly or annually for the foreseeable future. My parents' home church, where my father had been a pastor for the previous five and a half years, generously agreed to continue paying my father while allowing him to spend half of his time raising support, and the church also agreed to provide a significant monthly contribution. Over the next year, my parents were able to raise the majority of their support, though they did leave for the Philippines slightly underfunded and had to budget carefully.

The natural ebb and flow of life and economics meant that the list of givers providing for my family was perpetually in flux. People lost jobs, had new financial obligations, or died. In order to maintain enough income to sustain our family, my parents planned support trips back to the United States every fifth year. These yearlong furloughs followed the same basic pattern.

Each journey started with months of feverish preparation. Dad made arrangements for our housing in the Philippines, which meant anything from ending a lease to finding a house sitter and temporary places for our vehicles and dogs. We crammed most of our possessions into brilliant blue or red fifty-five gallon barrels and stored them in a warehouse along with our furniture. Meanwhile, Mother planned out a year's worth of academic material and packed it along with plenty of clothing, though our American friends and churches would help us acquire winter wardrobes once we arrived stateside.

The drive to Manila, from where we would fly to the U.S., took about a day. A portion of the highway between had a local nickname that meant "chicken intestines" because of the way it zigzagged through mountain switchbacks. Once in the capital city, we might have to spend a morning or two in the embassy, insuring that our passports and visas were shipshape, or the Filipino government would not allow us to leave the country. On some occasions expediting the paperwork meant paying people on the side, though this was a little different than bribery as nothing illegal was being proposed; sometimes the only way to insure that legal procedures went as they were supposed to was to encourage the right parties to do their job quickly. Then we waited for the main stage of the trip to begin.

I remember Dad waking us children on the mornings of our flights. It was normal for him to have been up most of the night finalizing packing and insuring that our luggage weighed the correct amount. We loaded into a van along with a couple of taxies and caravanned through streets that were only empty during the infant hours of the morning. When we arrived at the airport, we unloaded our luggage onto carts and stood in check-in lines for hours. Then we waited by our gate until our plane boarded.

Our first flight lasted two or three hours, ending at Tokyo or Osaka. We disembarked and wove our way through the airport, trying to find our next flight as an alternating cycle of Japanese, English, and other languages broadcasted through the intercom system, doubtless attempting to bestow order but only adding to the commotion. My parents and the older children all carried backpacks or laptops, and everyone but the youngest children pulled rolling luggage along. Eventually, we escaped through a departure gate, though the next phase was the most testing part of the trip.

For the subsequent thirteen hours, we sat in the belly of a 747 while we flew over the Pacific Ocean, and we could only hope that, like Jonah, we'd be vomited out at our destination. The only light came through the tiny windows along the ribcage of the plane, but they were slammed shut just after takeoff. The darkness helped the passengers sleep or watch the movies, though it is my personal opinion that airlines hold an annual competition to see which airline can showcase the worst selection of cinema. As a child, I felt like a caged animal; when claustrophobia set in, I'd slip into the aisle and pace up and down.

Normally the family sat together, but several of us wound up beside strangers. On one occasion, I sat beside a particularly large individual who filled up most of her seat and spilled over into mine—the bright side was that I did not need a pillow. I also didn't have to worry about throwing away any of my food, which was nice because the superb quality of airline food only adds to the general aura of delight. In my years of air travel, I learned one lesson about airplane food: airlines typically offer two varieties of food, an American and a foreign option. It is beneficial to choose the exotic cuisine because you don't know how that food is supposed to taste.

Our arrival in Minneapolis, Minnesota typically provided our first sense of the climate change; my family was dressed for the Philippines, so the walk through the jet way and into the terminal was frigid. We retrieved our checked luggage, waded through customs with Dad clutching a fistful of passports, rechecked our luggage, and then rushed to our next gate.

The third flight was easier than the first two, but we were far from finished. Layovers in Memphis, Tennessee were sedate enough; we felt relief at the nearness of the end of our journey, even if our emotions were clouded by a sleep-addled haze. By this point, Nathan was too weary to cause mischief, and we tried to find edible food for an affordable price before boarding our last flight.

The final leg to Wichita was blanketed in relief and exhaustion. Dark shadows marked the spans under our eyes, and dehydration manifested itself through incessant headaches, though dehydration at least meant fewer awkward treks down the airplane aisle to the bathroom. As we neared Wichita, all we wanted was a shower, a decent meal, and a toilet that couldn't suck a child in.

After the plane landed and we gathered our carry-ons, my family collected in the aisle, and one of the parents or older siblings gave some form of motivating speech before we stepped out onto stage. It went something like this: "We know you're tired. We all are. But the people waiting for us in the airport haven't seen us in years. Be on your best behavior."

Then we dragged ourselves down the exit tunnel, toward the concourse and were engulfed by strangers who knew our names but little else about us children. I imagine we looked like ostriches venturing out of a semi truck after days of travel, wide eyes bobbing back and forth, legs unsteady, plumage adroop. There were grandparents and my parents' friends with their kids, whom we were supposed to like immediately. There were some people too who started their greetings with things like, "Oh, I used to change your diapers when you were little."

Many of the faces were foreign at first glance yet bore a trace of the familiar. Everyone chattered away at once and seemed to forget that my family had basic needs and luggage to retrieve. Sometimes my siblings or I would sneak off to a restroom where it was quiet, though American bathrooms were disturbingly shiny. Eventually, the commotion wound down, the crowd shuffled toward the baggage claim, everyone dragged our belongings out to the parking lot, and we drove to the house that would serve as our residence for the year.

The theatrics fully commenced after we settled. Visiting the circuit of churches that supported my parents was the first priority, though the exact number of churches was constantly changing. When we visited a church, my family was expected to sit in the first few pews; my siblings and I were always conscious of eyes scrutinizing our every move. Between the music and sermon, the pastor would invite our family forward, and we would ascend the stage and line up in the spotlight while the pastor attempted to recall all of our names. If the church was small, Dad might step into the center ring and give the sermon.

After the service, we mingled with the natives, taking care that our behavior was saintly and appropriate for missionary kids. There was no playing hide-and-seek indoors or pilfering the communion wine. Sometimes there were potlucks, and we were expected to go first in line, which was problematic because the menu, with selections like baked beans, potato salad, and a variety of casseroles, was foreign to the younger kids. Not only did we have to guess at dishes, we had to gauge how much food we could procure without seeming gluttonous—skinny children do elicit better funding than obese ones.

While the rigorous routine of being introduced to new churches usually only lasted for the first few months of our furlough, we still attended multiple churches throughout the year. On any given weekend, we might be present for a Saturday night service, go elsewhere for an early Sunday morning service, and attend a third church before noon (for the longest time, I thought being late to church must be a sin). The most memorable part of church presentations occurred during the missions emphasis weekends. Many of our churches held annual mission fairs where the foyers were filled with colorful booths staffed by different missionaries. There were picture boards, foreign flags, and fliers, all held down by exotic trinkets and picture frames full of foreign currency, not to mention candy.

While most missionaries were content to stick close to their respective attractions, my family with our superior numbers employed a different tactic. Each kid took a stack of postcards, with our family and mission information, and a clip-board and waited until each service ended. As soon as the doors to the sanctuary opened and people started to stream out, we were among them, wolves among sheep, crafty as serpents but innocent as doves.

We attempted to make eye contact, briefly explain who we were, give them our family picture, and ask them to sign up to receive our monthly letter. Missionaries with longer contact lists for their monthly letters are almost invariably better funded, and my parents maintained well over a thousand names and addresses. Competition between my siblings ran rampant as we attempted to acquire the longest list of names, and many of the laity, once approached, learned to carry their postcard before them like a shield least they be stopped multiple times by different siblings. In order to provide additional motivation, Dad promised a buffet dinner if we collected enough signatures. Incidentally, Anna first met her husband during a missions fair, although she was so preoccupied with manning the booth that she was oblivious to his advances.

Only half of our family's financial support came from churches; the other half came from individuals and families. Some of these people were friends of my parents or seemingly random acquaintances while others decided to start funding our ministry after reading our newsletter for months or years. When my parents knew someone who they thought would consider partnering with them, my parents invited them over for dinner. Hosting allowed potential supporters the chance to hear about ministry in the Philippines, but it also served a deeper purpose.

The first concern most Christians had about our family doing mission work abroad was that there were too many of us. Could my parents negotiate the language barrier, lead Bible studies, preach sermons, appoint elders, diffuse church conflicts, and raise nine children concurrently? If only for an evening, dinner allowed interested people to venture behind the curtain and into the lions' den. The experience invariably removed all doubts.

Our guests usually arrived to discover the boys setting the table while Anna and the younger girls finished the meal preparations, leaving Dad and Mom free to entertain in the living room. During the meal, the kids kept quiet as the adults deliberated about mission work. Then the older girls served dessert. Afterward, the kids requested to be dismissed, cleared the table, and the boys cleaned the kitchen. The grown-ups moved back to the living room to watch a short film Dad had put together capturing the culture of the Philippines and the spiritual climate. The older kids helped the children prepare for bed, presenting them to say goodnight before retiring. When potential financial partners were present, we functioned as a flawless family unit, the wolf living with the lamb, the leopard lying down with the goat.

Still, not all aspects of furlough were performed flawlessly. My father was involved with the Rotary Club in the Philippines, successfully using the organization as a networking tool to build friendships with local Filipinos. One furlough, my father continued his involvement with Rotary by joining the branch in Wichita, Kansas, perhaps hoping that as he built relationships some individuals would be interested in becoming supporters.

That Christmas, the Rotary Club held a party at a local hotel. Upon their arrival at the hotel, Dad and Mom were directed down the correct hallway and noticed the menu they'd registered for being served. They slipped into the room and struck up a conversation with a doctor and his wife. However, part way through the meal, the emcee strode over to the podium, and started his address:

"Welcome to the Annual University of Kansas Medical School Christmas Party." Then with a smile in my parents' direction he added, "If that's not why you're here, we're glad you came anyway."

As it turned out, the Rotary party was in the room next door. Still, one of the doctors started supporting my parents a few years later; he probably figured they needed all the help they could get.

During furloughs, my family also hosted support banquets, which served as the grand finale. Months in advance, my parents started planning the venue, catering, and spectacle, while inviting current or prospective donors to attend and estimating the number of reservations. Normally, the event took place in an expansive indoor facility spread with linen-covered tables, chairs and a stage.

Each presentation was basically the same: Dad gave the opening address, the family sang a few songs, and the kids performed a choreographed poem about the Old Testament. Dinner was served as the main speaker elaborated on the plight of peoples living abroad with little or no knowledge of Jesus. Somewhere during the acts, Dad explained our ministry in the Philippines and gave an invitation to join our financial team. Crowds ran into the hundreds.

Once, we even added a board with a giant thermometer chart projecting our respective financial goals for monthly support and one-time giving. Throughout the evening, people handed their pledge cards to my siblings who attended the tables, we informed Enoch of the amount, and he painted in the progress. With each new commitment the red stripe ascended, and it was natural to wonder if a buzzer and lights would go off if somehow the crimson strip reached the top, or maybe someone would win a giant teddy bear. I never found out because the giving eventually petered off.

Support banquets tended to be a magnet for extreme circumstances. For instance, it was right before this particular fundraiser that Enoch was expelled from high school. Unbeknownst to Dad and Mom, he bought a *balisong*—a Filipino butterfly knife—at a local retailer since he owned one in the Philippines. He carried it around with him, practicing opening and closing techniques, not realizing that the balisong was considered a switchblade and illegal to carry in Kansas. One day, Enoch forgot to remove the knife from his pocket before he left for school. In his drama class, Enoch volunteered to act out a scene, and the balisong fell out of his pocket during the performance. The instructor asked for the knife, Enoch complied, and he went on with his classes. An hour later, however, the police showed up. They handcuffed Enoch and drove him to the juvenile detention center where the authorities called my father.

Enoch was released upon my father's arrival, but the damage was done. Because he was a minor, Enoch's criminal record would be expunged within the next year. Nevertheless, the local high school had a zero-tolerance policy because it was plagued by gang violence; the school had red lockers, and the local joke was that the color was chosen to hide blood stains. Enoch was promptly expelled.

The expulsion meant that Nic would lose an entire year and a half of school. Our family immediately started the appeal procedure, but it was a long, protracted process requiring interviews and letters from Enoch's teachers, not to mention consultations with the principle, a meeting with the school board, and the final decision from the superintendent. Chances were slim. It looked like an impossible situation.

The expulsion happened in the weeks leading up to our support banquet. My parents concurrently pursued a speaker and caterers and made other necessary arrangements while praying about Enoch's situation and what should be done after the banquet was finished. In the end, Don Richardson flew in to be the main speaker, and the dinner was a success, arguably the best we ever had, even though we still had more support to raise afterward. Nic was still out of school at the time of the banquet. Afterwards, my parents talked with friends about the issue and moved forward with the appeal process.

The school board voted unanimously to reinstate Enoch, based largely on the glowing letters his teachers provided and his impeccable academic record. He was able to finish out the semester. When Mom, who diligently recorded our family life in her journals, counted up the number of days from Enoch's expulsion to his restoration, she found something peculiar: The expulsion lasted for forty days, a number in the Bible that is associated with testing. For example, the rain during Noah's flood lasted forty days, the Israelites wandered in the desert for forty years, and Jesus was tested in the desert for forty days. While my parents did not belabor the point, they also did not forget.

At the end of each furlough, my family packed up our scant belongings. Our churches made sure to call us onto stage and pray for us. We said goodbye to old and new friends while savoring the last elements of the American climate—the blue sky, the clean air, the litter-free sidewalks. At the beginning of the year, most of my siblings and I didn't want to go to America; by the end of the year, we didn't wanted to leave America. Still, we always left.

Christmas in July

While living in the Philippines, my family didn't experience an autumn prelude to Christmas accompanied by a few weeks of frigid temperatures as winter settled in. Because the country is situated along the equator, the weather in the Philippines scarcely changes during the latter months of the year. There were no snow storms, no fires to keep the living room comfortable, and for that matter no chimneys for Santa to squeeze down. The flora retained its plumage, and the humidity trickled down our backs like melted butter.

Still, it was Christmas. Without Thanksgiving to mark the beginning of the season, in the Filipino mindset Christmas started with the "ber" months: September, October, November, and December. Decorations, like the colorful stars constructed out of bamboo strips and paper, graced buildings and trees. Without a fireplace, we hung our stockings in the kitchen, and our Christmas tree was artificial. However, there was never any shortage of presents. With eleven members in our family, there was always a sprawling pile under the tree that spilled into the room.

The gifts from our supporting churches doubled the number. Most years, in July, one of our supporting churches placed the names of their missionaries and their children on Christmas trees in the lobby. Members of the congregation took a name and bought a present for that individual. Sometimes the giver knew the person and made a point of selecting that same name each year, though most of the time the selection was random. The gifts for each missionary family were boxed up and shipped a good five months before Christmas, in hopes that they would somehow arrive at their destination by the holidays, despite the abysmal foreign postal services.

The extra gifts meant my family ended up with more presents than we could open in an organized fashion on Christmas Eve, so two or three days before Christmas, each of us children got to select a present to unwrap early. This was necessary because my family opened one present at a time—I think to develop the patience of the children. This also enabled my mother to record every gift so thank you notes could be written, and it curbed the sugar high due to the sudden influx of American candy included with the presents.

Before opening the remaining presents on Christmas Eve, we ate at a restaurant, and then we drove around Naga City perusing the Christmas lights. When we arrived back at the house, we unloaded the stockings that had magically filled while we were out—though Dad and Mom rather suspiciously had to go in before the kids to check and make sure Santa had come—and unwrapping presents lasted until midnight.

Christmas Day was low key, with the traditional American holiday dinner. The turkey, cranberry sauce, black olives, and dill and okra pickles were all bought in Manila weeks before and flown or driven the remaining hundreds of kilometers southeast. The mashed potatoes, gravy, and stuffing were all made by hand, as box mixes were not readily accessible; the pies were likewise homemade.

We'd sit down at the table, and inevitably someone would tell the story about a missionary child who went back to America for the holidays: He sat at the table, surrounded by family and a host of American dishes, with a forlorn expression on his face. His grandmother leaned over and asked, "Are you okay? What would you like to eat?"

The boy replied, "Grandmother, what I'd really like is some fish eye soup."

I always empathized with the kid; I couldn't understand the appeal of Thanksgiving and Christmas food. The flavors were rather bland, and there was nothing exotic about the food—no pig heads, no chicken feet, no snails. I believe to this day that a holiday is only as exciting as its cuisine.

No Christmas would be complete without carolers, and the Philippines provided no shortage of them, though their mentality was slightly different. Rather than circulating throughout the neighborhood with the intent of blessing others and spreading good cheer, most Filipino carolers consisted of roving bands of boys who went from house to house shrilling whatever lyrics they could remember at the moment until someone gave them candy. These caroling groups were, on principle, tone deaf, and I hold that people gave them candy simply to shut them up.

Afterward the boys would nonsensically croon,

Thank you very much
Thank you very much
Thank you for your Merry Christmas.

However, if the candy was tardy, they would sing instead,

We are waiting for
We are waiting for
We are waiting for your Christmas.

If the candy still did not arrive, some of the boys might opt to throw rocks at windows or decorations—in the spirit of the season of course. In the end, the experience was more reminiscent of trick-or-treating than caroling, the choruses more ghoulish than saintly, but then, I suppose Filipinos don't celebrate Halloween.

Sometimes during caroling season, Enoch and I snuck outside our house and waited for carolers to come by and start screeching. When one of our katulongs, Anna, or Caleb came out to distribute candy, all the boys thrust their hands through the bars of our gate. Hoping to get some, Enoch and I hid in the throng and stuck our hands out as well. However, our scheme never worked as our skin was woefully, conspicuously porcelain white set against dark skin and shadows. Often enough, the candy dealer placed something sticky or rotten in our hands instead.

Most years in the Philippines my family held our annual Gray International Christian Academy Christmas Party—Gray International Christian Academy was the name my parents used for our home school, though most of us simply used the acronym G.I.C.A. At the time, home schooling was increasing in popularity in the U.S., but the concept was a complete novelty in the Philippines where only the financially destitute educated their children at home.

Especially since they had a large family and time was normally in short supply, my parents often combined ministry with home schooling. For instance, we sent out a newsletter to our supporters and friends stateside every several months, and my siblings and I wrote several of the articles. The writing provided fresh perspective for our readers while developing the student. In the same way, my parents discovered that home schooling provided a mechanism to reach the Filipino community. Many locals refused to visit a Bible study led by born-again Christians. However, they were curious and excited about attending a home school Christmas party.

Our first party started out small enough. We held it at our house and fit the guests into our living and dining rooms. The children recited the story of Jesus' birth in Matthew 1:18-25. Dad and Anna sang "White Christmas" with Mom accompanying on the piano. Meanwhile several of us children stood on the stairs overhead tossing shredded pieces of Styrofoam—a sight more reminiscent of dandruff than snow. Mom discussed the home school process, and Dad spoke about Jesus.

Each year the party expanded: We added extra seating and began serving a meal; the program grew to include poetry recitations and a Christmas skit. The number of guests swelled until one year we rented a ballroom at a local hotel. Sometimes when Dad spoke about Jesus, people made spiritual decisions. Other times guests became interested in Bible studies, having witnessed that this American family was unusual and willing to share but not dangerous or liable to force some kind of conversion.

One home school celebration was more memorable than those of other years. My family invited more guests than our house could fit, so we decided to hold the party outdoors. We set up lights, rented chairs and tables, and catered a fancy meal, only to discover that we'd made one oversight: monsoon season in the Philippines that year lasted into December. It rained every day. The concrete driveway beside and behind our house, the planned center of the event, grew a layer of moss that turned slick with even a light amount of precipitation.

Our family prayed for dry weather. As the day of the party grew closer, however, the rain didn't abate. We positioned the buffet under our carport, so people could serve themselves outside and wander inside without getting wet. Holding the program inside would be far from ideal though; with so many bodies close together, the space would heat to a simmering temperature.

The day before the party, the weather was dry. Since there were still puddles of water on our driveway, several of my family members scrubbed the moss loose and swept the green amalgam away so the concrete could dry. The next day, we set up the furniture and sound system as the caterers prepared the food. All the while, we kept a nervous eye on the sky.

Guests started arriving on time, which in the Philippines meant most of them were at least half an hour late. The cuisine was excellent and abundant with dishes like Bicol Express, a popular food with pork, shrimp, and coconut milk. The songs, poems, and speeches elicited laughter or solemnity at the appropriate moments, and several Filipinos made decisions to follow Jesus. In particular, the wives of a couple judges made significant steps in their spiritual journey. The festivities lasted late into the night. Eventually the final visitors left, and the cleanup began.

Thirty minutes later, it started to rain.

In the wake of the annual party and Christmas, my family usually slipped away to a beach for a few days. The settings were beautiful: coastlines strewn with white or black sand, streams meandering their way to the sea, palm trees with coconuts, and tidal islands. Below the waves, the sand was strewn with starfish, sea urchins, and coral; neon fish darted along and around and through the castles on the ocean floor while transparent jelly fish drifted in the currents.

Still adventure always comes with risk. In retrospect, I wonder sometimes how any mother could find days along the ocean shore with nine children tranquil. There were riptides and snakes; the water was a source of great pleasure and potential fear. Mother monitored our whereabouts, and each of us siblings remained aware of the others too; the elder siblings were responsible for the middle kids while Mother focused the majority of her attention on the youngest children. Usually a katulong came along to help as well.

I remember days when the local fishermen ventured out in outrigger canoes, dropped their nets in giant circles, and returned hauling the ends of their ropes. People gathered along the shore and hauled in the nets for what seemed like hours, some standing on the bank and others wading up to their waist, the water rushing around their legs, the muscles on shoulders and backs straining under the sunlight.

My siblings and I sometimes waded in among the nationals and added our childish strength to theirs. The end of the nets finally floated into the shallows, and the men dragged it onto the beach, a tangled network of ropes and cords dancing with fish, crawling with crabs and writhing with other sea creatures. The fishermen descended on the catch, dividing its contents in a flurry.

On those late December days, the sun rose and set, time no longer a currency. We played in the sun and the shadows, the sand alternately hot or cool under our feet, the ocean water warm or chilly. Meal times fluctuated based on mood, and we snacked on fruits and chips in the interim. The nights ended with natural bedtimes; the mornings began without the sound of an alarm. It was like Eden along the ocean, with plenty of childish reminders that humanity is far from perfection.

After the break, we returned home for the New Year's celebration. Sidewalk venders appeared everywhere downtown selling a variety of fireworks: sparklers, fountains, an assortment of bottle rockets, mild firecrackers that were like black cats, and explosives called five stars that could ruin a man's hand. The fuses were homemade and unreliable. Most of the fireworks were illegal, but nobody, even the police, cared about the laws enough to change tradition.

Dad bought fireworks and other supplies for our celebration. New Year's Eve was one time when our parents splurged and bought things like Doritos or cheese, which were difficult to come by and expensive—the local substitute for cheese being a biological waste product called Quikmelt that, contrary to the name, did not melt and tasted as though it was fifty percent plastic. Normally, my family attended a local friend's party in the evening and returned home for a night filled with games and snacks.

The immaculate firework displays that Americans are accustomed to were absent, but neighborhoods made up for the lack of continuity and organization with sheer firepower. From dusk to late in the morning, the sky was dotted with rockets, white fingers stabbing into the darkness, and the heavens were a mass of repercussions. Our eardrums echoed from the violence of the assaults, and one never knew when or where to expect the next massive detonation. In the morning when the air was finally still, there would be a layer of gunpowder on the floor of our house, even though the shutters had all been shut tight.

Inundated

In the Philippines, the relaxed tropical year is drowned by typhoon season. It was only while monitoring storms that local broadcasting stations showcased the weather, and suddenly people who scarcely noticed the climate tuned in with fervor. My family didn't watch television or listen to the radio, so I learned to predict typhoons by observing the Filipinos.

Before each tempest, one of the first indicators was the change in dress; as the temperature dipped perhaps as low as the 70's the Filipinos donned winter jackets, lest they freeze. Downtown Naga City became frenzied with the flood of shoppers preparing for the storm, and prices spiked. People stocked up on canned goods, batteries, flashlights, candles, and drinking water. Gas stations ran out of fuel as people topped off their vehicles or bought gasoline for their generators. Alcohol sales soared as some people bought the depressant to help relieve the trials of the impending torrent. Many of them believed that the alcohol would keep them warm—of course the only thing better than experiencing a natural disaster is doing so drunk.

Rice farmers waited until they were certain the typhoon was going to plow through the area before they rushed into the fields, with all their family members and every available friend, and harvested the juvenile rice—better an immature crop than none at all. Then quiet. All but the bravest tricycle and jeepney drivers abandoned their routes, the city became a ghost town, and people closed themselves within their homes and battened down the windows, waiting in the calm for the worst.

The wind shifted almost imperceptibly at first. The cloud cover thickened until the sky writhed and boiled over with moisture, wrestling with the dropping temperatures. The wind raced along empty roads and ripped leaves from trees. Next the rain: a drizzle at first and then a deluge drenching the earth with raindrops falling like bullets. In the wonder of it all, in the power of the moment, time itself disappeared, a construct of consciousness now secondary to instincts more primal.

I would sit inside, my thoughts in the doldrums, listening to the drumming as the rain beat along our metal roof and the screaming of the wind as it ripped along outside. With our shutters and doors closed, the air inside didn't move; our body heat regulated the temperatures inside the concrete boundaries of our home.

Within the first few hours, we discovered the spots where our roof leaked. Normally the ribbed metal sheets nailed to our roof shed the water with little trouble, but typhoon winds could drive the rain horizontally and blow it up under the layers, where it dripped down the rafters. Little puddles seeped through our ceiling and dripped into the buckets we arranged to subdue the mess.

Water intruded at other points as well. Sometimes, my family watched the flood rise within inches of our entry doors, even though at the same time it was pouring out our front gate. I remember on more than one occasion, spending hours mopping up the water that the wind blew under our doors. We even had boards and sandbags for each entranceway in case the situation grew dire.

Because of the potential for floods in the Philippines, people consider where water will flow when buying a house. In a property search, even immaculate houses are often discarded if they rest in the path of typhoon waters. Consequently, most middle or upper-class homes are built closer to mountains.

For many Filipinos, however, this option simply isn't affordable, so every typhoon season they watch their house flood. Belongings are moved in advance, hopefully to a second story if the house has one. After the inundation, the lower levels are cleaned and set in order again. A house across from one of our residences in the Philippines inexplicably had a basement—a necessity in Kansas because of tornadoes but an oddity in the tropics. Every typhoon season the lower level transformed into a cistern for weeks at a time rendering the space completely useless, except as a fishery or refuge for pythons or crocodiles.

Once you were in a typhoon, you couldn't do a whole lot to contain the water or resist the wind. Then in the middle of the torrent of wind and water, at the height of each storm, everything suddenly stopped. The precipitation halted, the wind calmed, and the clouds lightened. It wasn't the end though, just half-time—the eye of the storm. I never got over the irony of it all, that in the midst of the worst there could be serenity, but often life isn't a matter of finding a peace devoid of trials; instead it's a matter of finding tranquility in the heart of the tempest.

As a teenager, I liked to venture outside in the calm and experience the new world. The trees were bare; some were snapped in two or lay prostrate on the ground with roots, washed clean of soil, dangling in the air. Typhoon season is the only Fall the tropics experiences, and all the leaves underfoot were green and fresh and protested the violence of their abduction.

Nearby rice fields, which often rested in an inch of water, were drowned in runoff, with only little hills and ridges of dirt showing. The nearby ponds had rushed past their boundaries; the street in front of our house was a stream. Little spotted gouramis, along with other tropical fish, darted along the current, and I once watched a man trudge through the water coursing down the street and kill a catfish with a machete.

When I wandered around our house, I spotted the places where the sewers had overflowed because there were intrusions of cockroaches huddled along the wall with their antennae twitching. No creature in all my childhood abroad evoked as much horror and revulsion as the Asian cockroach. These roaches were unlike the Midwest variety, which were small and earthbound.

In addition to being two inches long and able to fly, the Asian brand of cockroach is virtually indestructible. Mother once caught a roach trekking across the kitchen floor and stepped on it, but the bug continued on. As you would expect, Mom stamped on it a second and third time, but the insect kept going. Finally, Mother stomped on the cockroach so vigorously that she ruptured a blood vessel in her leg. Still the roach meandered away. In time, we learned to swat the cockroaches with a flyswatter, scoop them up, and flush them down the toilet.

Even as I studied the quiet, drowned world outside, the weather would shift again. The deluge resumed, the wind and rain fierce as ever before. As the storm wore on, the leaking and flooding worsened, and almost every storm was accompanied by electrical failure. Cables and poles toppled over, or there were problems at the power plant. Often enough, the companies shut off the power preemptively, electricity and water being an imprudent combination. These power outages, or brownouts as they are referred to in the Philippines, lasted for hours or entire days at a time. Without electricity, the days seemed shorter than ever and the nights quite dreary.

For those who could afford them, residential generators filled the void. Our family generator was stored around the side of our house and could be connected to the building's power grid in a few minutes. The electrical current was limited but enabled our family to use a small number of appliances.

Once, when I was a teenager, my parents were away on business in Manila, and one of our katulongs and I were in charge of the household. News of an impending typhoon arrived, and we made all the necessary preparations. After the first few hours of the typhoon, I started watching the 2002 rendition of *The Count of Monte Cristo*, starring Jim Caviezel and Guy Pearce.

I had never seen the film before and was intrigued from the opening scene: I was charmed by Edmond Dantes, enchanted by Mercedes' beauty, and distraught with the injustice of Dantes's imprisonment. I breathed with the film in relief as Abbe Faria, brilliantly portrayed by Richard Harris, joined Dantes in his cell. Then Dantes' daring escape—at which point the power went out. I was left sitting in total darkness, the anticipation dangling me from my heartstrings.

I was in no position to resolve myself to wait until the power returned, likely days later, before I learned the end to the story. Instead, I grabbed my flip-flops, unlocked the outside doors, and strode into the soaking, inky blackness outside where I flipped breakers and prepared the system for use of our generator. Next, I sloshed through ankle deep water to our generator, which was damp but out of the water's reach. After filling the tank with gasoline, I turned the generator on and sloshed back inside where I was able to finish the movie. Whatever risk of electrocution I ran was for a worthy cause, and the film is one of my favorites to this day.

The danger of theft and looters was another liability that followed the typhoons. My family's first generator was stolen on one occasion, despite being chained and padlocked down.

Later on, my family built an entire concrete structure to protect our generator, complete with a wrought iron gate, thicker chains, additional padlocks, and a partition to conceal it from sight. Concern about looting was prevalent for many people as thieves used the chaos to steal whatever could be carried off, including items like propane tanks.

After a typhoon ended, everything was quiet, as if nature had exhausted its capacity for destruction and sunk into lethargy. The town was transformed; many of the areas were flooded to the extent that roads were no longer visible, and people paddled from one location to the next in canoes as if Naga City was suddenly a tropical Venice.

The romance of it all was lost in the destruction that remained. Buildings were damaged, some beyond repair, with roofs taking an especially hard toll. Food existed as a primary need; the marketplaces opened again, but provisions were low and prices elevated by demand and the constricted supply lines. For weeks or even months many types of produce, particularly bananas, remained scarce. Likewise, seafood vanished from menus as the onslaught of the typhoon had ravaged the ocean floor, and fishermen slaved to repair their equipment.

In the following days, news stations recounted stories of the destruction both on local and national scales. The number of fatalities frequently mounted into the hundreds or higher, many deaths the result of drowning or landslides or starvation. For me as a child, the news was not as shocking as it might have been to most American kids. People died in natural disasters in the Philippines all the time. Though more rare, there were multiple volcanic eruptions when I was growing up as a child, and people frequently died of exotic diseases or terrorist attacks.

Even when I was in the U.S.A. on furloughs, news about tragedy did not have the same effect on me that it had on others.

Even the bombing of the World Trade Center on September 11 did not impact me with the same level of anguish many Americans felt. In a similar way, the destruction of Hurricane Katrina left me unfazed—even after I spent a week in New Orleans helping with hurricane relief. In my mind, such calamity was not uncommon. The world was not an inherently peaceful place; death was a reality. People died or lost their livelihoods all the time, and life went on.

In many ways, experiencing typhoon season was like living in a water park where you traverse the same ride over and over again. There's the calm before the plunge, the instant before you push off in your inner tube. Then you're away. All around there is wind and water, twists and turns and free falls. Each loop takes you lower and lower until finally you shoot out of the chaos onto a pond covered with water so muddy that you can't see more than a few inches deep.

Outside the current caused by the slide, the water is tranquil, yet you can't escape the feeling that somewhere under the calm, underneath the smooth surface, there are dead bodies drifting along, victims of the amusement. You never know when you might brush up against one. Still the routine becomes so customary that it grows mundane, even ordinary, and you forget the eerie sensation entirely, oblivious to what exists a breath away.

Among Our Kind

For my siblings and me, growing up in the Philippines for most of our lives didn't mean we fit in. When we'd played in our yard, the neighborhood children often passed along the street outside or stood at our fence peering in. Some asked us questions or tried to make conversation, and others taunted us or made obscene gestures, as if we were animals in a zoo. Eventually we learned to ignore the disturbances, but they were a constant reminder that we were different.

There was one time a year when my family escaped the scrutiny of living in the Philippines as Caucasians. It was called Annual Field Conference. For one week, the missionaries with Regions Beyond Missionary Union (RBMU), who were located in the Philippines, joined together. The adults spent hours in meetings, but the kids made crafts and played games all day long. For me, AFC was a time of festivity and one of the few occasions when I interacted with Americans, particularly Americans my own age.

While there were other locations, the site for AFC that I remember the most was Caliraya Re-Creation Center. Built both as a vacation setting and a spot for business conferences, camp Caliraya bore strong western influences, including expansive, manicured lawns and air-conditioning. Built alongside a lake that required guests to be ferried from the parking lot to the camp grounds, the resort featured a host of leisure activities, from fishing to jet skiing.

Caliraya's manager was a man named Joe Mauk. He owned a collection of tops from around the globe. During his top shows, he demonstrated his favorite tops and tricks, spinning them on his hand or on other tops, bouncing them off his shoe, flipping them around his back or through his legs. He had a top made of mahogany and another one so big that it had to be wound up with a rope and dropped from a coconut tree. Each stunt came with a narrative that he used as a part in sharing the gospel. When Mr. Mauk wasn't directing the resort staff or troubleshooting, he was interacting with the guests and telling tales.

The dining hall at Caliraya offered something rare for the Philippines: a buffet. Massive piles of food were heaped in giant metal containers with a variety of entrees, soups, and dinner rolls; there was even a coffee stand and tables reserved for dessert. Servers rotated among the tables refilling glasses and taking special requests. It was lucky that meal times were limited or Annual Field Conference would have been an exercise in gluttony.

The camp had rustic cabins with communal bathrooms, but most guests stayed in the main lodge—a massive structure that rested on top of a ridge. The building had a triangular base, four tiers, and a tower; the shape reminded me of a cruise ship. From the lookout, one could gaze across the resort during the day and see the distant lake beach. At night the stars gleamed against an inky sky.

Our first AFC conference at Caliraya took place while construction of the tower was still underway; the bare concrete and exposed rebar made the place feel like a medieval castle. That year, our conference week fell on the 4th of July, and we celebrated the American holiday by shooting off fireworks from the top of the hill.

Another year, I remember several of the missionary children building extension cords. I'm not sure whose brilliant idea that was—kids and electrical current make such a judicious combination. The project did have some merit, however, as extension cords were rarely available in Filipino stores. Since the electrical current in the Philippines was 220 volts instead of 110, importing American extension cords wasn't a simple solution.

So a bunch of missionary kids ended up splicing wires, attaching plugs or sockets, and testing our trade skills. At the end, each child plugged a fan into his extension cord and plugged the cord into the wall. One missionary kid forgot to let go of his cord before someone turned the fan on; his wiring was faulty, and as the electrical current ran up his fingers, he hollered, "Ttuurrrrn it offff!"

From an adolescent age on, one of the primary draws AFC had for me was the romantic potential. Most of the girls I interacted with on a daily basis were Filipino. Many of them were attractive, with their dark hair and slanted eyes, and they paid plenty of special attention to me that resulted in a parade of crushes. Outside of AFC, I, like my brothers, was the subject of many shy smiles and whispered conversations.

Those connections were tricky though. I realized that most of the attention I received was due to my being an American. Young Filipinas automatically perceived me as attractive and wealthy. I wanted to be desirable because of who I was as an individual, not because of my nationality and economic status. Besides, there was a disparity between me and most of these girls and a lack of common ground: we came from distinct family backgrounds, had different educational experiences, possessed different tastes, and didn't share the same first language.

Annual Field Conference allowed me to socialize with girls who had traits that were similar to mine; they were missionary kids, most of them were Caucasian, and they had a western education. Naturally, this meant many conference weeks were filled with juvenile flirting and crushing heartbreaks. To my dismay, the boys usually outnumbered the girls, and many girls tended to like older boys while I preferred girls closer to my age or even older. The vast majority of the time, nothing came of those interactions; most girls were probably oblivious to my interest anyway, and I left as single as I arrived. Nonetheless, it was something to look forward to every year.

The most iconic element of the Annual Field Conference was the night when people presented funny skits and competed for prizes. One year our national director participated in a skit where he dressed up as a woman, complete with a skirt and padded brazier. On another occasion, there was a competition where kids and parents tried to recreate a comic familial moment. Instead of the family members portraying themselves, the roles were shuffled; the parents played the kids and the kids the parents.

That year, my family reenacted what often happened during our evenings. Normally we would read books like the *Chronicles of Narnia* or *The Lord of the Rings*. Many of those readings ended in the same fashion.

Sitting in a chair on stage, Enoch as the thespian of the family took upon himself the role of Mother. Meanwhile Mother and the rest of the kids sat around the chair portraying the teenagers and younger children in our family. Nic began the act by yawning as he read a few lines from a book, eventually stopping after he read, "'The city will be destroyed.'"

At this point he nodded to sleep while the other family members poked each other and smirked. Then Enoch jerked back awake. He looked at the book again and resumed reading, "'The city will be destroyed.'" Then he asked, "Wait, did I read that already?"

"Yes, Mom," we answered.

"Oh, okay. 'The city will be destroyed... the city will be destroyed,'" he trailed off.

"Mom, we can read another time. You can rest."

"No. No. I'm fine. Really. Where were we? Oh yes." Enoch squinted and looked at the page, backed up all the way to the beginning of the paragraph, and started again, finally getting back to the line where he'd stopped. "'The city... the city will be destroyed... the city that Gaal is in will be destroyed.'" There was a hint of smugness in his voice at finishing the whole sentence. But almost immediately Enoch's head started to loll to one side, and the kids chorused, "Mom, go to bed."

At Annual Field Conference, there was a tradition known as the *Sayang* Award—sayang being Tagalog for "what a pity." Competitors for the award recounted for the audience their saddest and funniest tale from the last year. The story of the missionary who threw his food out the window with a screen and my parents' experience going to the wrong Christmas party were both stores told in competitions for the Sayang Award—Dad and Mom won the award that conference.

The prize was awarded based on audience participation; after all the narratives were told, the emcee announced each entry and gave the audience time to answer "Sayang" after each one. The louder the response, the higher score the story received.

Even the kids participated in the story telling: a girl bemoaned how her pants got caught in her bike chain and were ripped off, right in front of a boy she liked. One young man shared how he accidently went to school in only a t-shirt and his boxers where his girlfriend pointed out the mistake. Another kid lamented his experience on a trampoline when his bouncing got out of control and his legs slipped between the springs; he added succinctly, "It hurt."

Still the adults told the best tales. One year, a single missionary lady in Manila relayed her experience while wandering around downtown. Someone uncovered a manhole without clearly marking the area. This woman didn't notice the gaping hole and fell in. Splattered with sewage, she finally got past the shock of the fall and began to climb out of the hole. When her head poked out the top, a local spotted her, hurried over and chided her saying, "Ma'am, you can't go down there." The lady won the Sayang Award that year, for falling down a manhole and coming out without a man.

On another occasion, a woman told about her experience making a shake. She peeled and cut the fruit, added the evaporated milk and sugar, blended the ingredients together, and added ice cubes. However, when she drank the shake, the taste was odd. Then she noticed pieces of house gecko in the mixture. Apparently a lizard fell from the ceiling and into the blender when she wasn't paying attention.

My favorite story though was told by a lady in language school. She learned words or phrases during the morning and ventured into the community later in the day to utilize her new vocabulary. To appreciate this story, it is necessary to understand one particular aspect of Filipino culture: in the Philippines, men pee indiscriminately. While stuck in Manila traffic one day, my father watched a bus driver step out of his bus and pee on his tire while stopped at a light. During road trips, men answer natures call within sight of the highway. Likewise, walls throughout cities become impromptu urinals, and as a result, many bear writing proclaiming "*Huwag umihi dito*"—Don't pee here.

On this particular day, the missionary lady was learning the word "*patingin*?" a term meaning, "May I look?" This question is frequently used when interacting with a vendor whose valuables one wants to inspect. Equipped with her new term, this woman visited a store but could not find the owner anywhere. Finally, she spotted a man facing the wall outside the building. Oblivious to what was happening, the woman walked straight up to the man and blurted, "Patingin?"

It was well into my teenage years before I began to understand the business side of Annual Field Conference. In the meantime though, it served a good purpose that I did recognize. It lets us missionary kids know that we weren't alone; there were others like us who were trying to figure out where they fit too. If nothing else, at least we blended better than the adults did.

The Return

To my parents, the Annual Mission Conference was hardly a vacation. They spent much of the week with agendas and addendums. The missionaries sat in seminars discussing Filipino culture, new Filipino government procedures, and changes within the mission or its policies. There were meetings during the day, followed by a few hours of free time. Then they had dinner and more meetings.

Some years, the missionaries elected new team leaders, both for the country and the regions where they were stationed. I can only imagine that the meetings, at times, fell into mock versions of the Republican and Democratic National Conventions, characterized by ceaseless debate. By the time the election was actually held, everyone was sick of the affair. Tensions could run high, and for my parents the days were exhausting, both of them being fairly introverted. Though parts of the conference were designed to rejuvenate and equip the missionaries, these activities were often designed by the extroverts in the team and appealed to group-oriented methods of recharging.

The situation at Annual Field Conferences became stringent when Regions Beyond Missionary Union merged with another organization. Among other changes, the new organization was not as supportive of large families; they had policies pertaining to pay allotment and number of children that favored small families. These and other adjustments intensified arguments that later arose within the team.

For instance, at some point, one group of missionaries in our field decided that only Bible study materials written in Filipino languages should be used in the church plants. This concerned various missionaries because it eliminated the vast amount of Christian literature available in English which many Filipinos understood. Some missionaries felt this was an attempt by other missionaries to force material that they had written on the rest of the team.

It should be noted that the official position of my parents' mission was to work in the vernacular of the target people. My parents felt that the mission was too rigid in this regard and failed to adequately embrace the unique environment of the Philippine islands. There had been a strong American presence in the Philippines for nearly one hundred years, and English was commonly used. Indeed, when the Department of Culture, Education, and Sports selected a language for use in colleges and universities, they chose English. These factors gave American missionaries the unusual privilege of being well accepted by the business and professional classes. My parents used English materials because this focus enabled them to uniquely target judges, lawyers, businessmen and women, teachers, bankers, and so forth. This reflected my parents' earlier training in the Campus Crusade for Christ ministry; Dr. Bill Bright would commonly say, "If we reach the campus today, we will reach the world tomorrow."

As issues like these continued, two major factions arose within our mission—I like to refer to them as the righteous minority and everyone else. Over time, members of the marginalized group, weary of the bickering, started leaving the mission field.

Before long, the size of our team shriveled. The experience was reminiscent of Paul's warning in Galatians 5:15, "If you bite and devour each other, watch out or you will be destroyed by each other."

As the conflicts built, my parents faced another challenge. When they had decided to become missionaries, many of my relatives did not easily accept that my family was moving to the other side of the world. At the time, my siblings were the only grandchildren on both sides of the family. My maternal grandparents were Methodist, and my paternal grandmother was an Episcopalian, which enabled them to understand the need for missionaries, though the idea of our family leaving was still challenging. My paternal grandfather, however, was not particularly religious, and Dad will never forget his father's response. Grandpa told him, "If you go to the Philippines as a missionary, that is your business. But if you leave and you take your wife and your children, you are a fool, and I will disown you." Those words resonated deeply in Dad's mind and heart, though he knew he could not stay just to please his father. Our family continued on the path to the Philippines.

Over the years, my parents struggled with a paradox: Jesus warns, in Luke 9:62, that, "No one who puts a hand to the plow and looks back is fit for service in the kingdom of God," while Paul, in 1 Timothy 5:8, cautions that, "Anyone who does not provide for their relatives, and especially for their own household, has denied the faith and is worse than an unbeliever." The former kept my parents from staying in the United States, even when my grandfather called Dad a fool. Yet seventeen years later, the latter prevented them from being at peace remaining in the Philippines.

My paternal grandmother contracted lung cancer. Since my dad's siblings were deceased, we felt a deep responsibility for grandmother. Anna had finished high school, so she agreed to return to the U.S. and live in Chanute where she aided my grandparents and attended the local junior college. When Grandmother went into remission, Anna returned to the Philippines. However, Grandmother developed compression fractures, and we did not know how bad she was. Unbeknownst to us, she came down with pneumonia and later died. We received word of her death the day after our Christmas party, the one where the Lord held back the rain. Dad was the only one who returned for the funeral because we couldn't afford to fly the whole family back.

The next child in line, Caleb, returned to the U.S. and stayed with Grandfather Gray for his junior college years. After Caleb transferred to a university, Enoch took his place in Chanute. Once Enoch was about to transfer to Prairie Bible Institute in Canada though, my parents were in a quandary; Grandpa Gray was in his mid-eighties, and mother's parents were elderly.

My parents began investigating stateside job opportunities as they continued to work abroad. My dad contemplated pastoral positions, and together my parents looked into ministries in the U.S.—all of this was accompanied by prayer. Before they went to the Philippines, Dad and Mom built a relationship with a missionary named Norm Allen who worked with an agency called International Students Incorporated, an organization that ministers to the international students who attend American colleges. Dad and Mom applied to join the ministry, were offered a position in Wichita, and accepted the job.

It wasn't a total surprise when my siblings and I found out that we were relocating to the U.S. We'd watched missionaries for most of our lives; they didn't stay on the same mission field forever. We'd seen a common pattern among other missionaries in the Philippines as their children aged. According to the experiences we'd witnessed, the older missionary kids got, the harder it was for their parents to stay in the mission field.

It's challenging for parents to pluck their children out of their home culture, drop them into a foreign environment, and observe them as they struggle to belong. This trial gets worse as the children grow past ages where they can easily be home schooled and the need for peer interaction intensifies. To compensate, many missionary families in the Philippines who started out in more remote regions would migrate to Manila where they could send their kids to Faith Academy, though some families like mine chose to board their teens instead.

It was commonly accepted among my siblings that once a family moved to Manila they would rarely remain in the Philippines for more than five years, though there were exceptions. Among other things, tuition was not cheap, and that added financial tension to stressful work. When our parents did decide to leave the Philippines, though, it still caught several of us off guard—leaving the mission field was something other families did. We thought our family was somehow going to defy the trend.

For me, especially, the news was heartbreaking because I'd been setting down deeper roots. As a teen, I was constantly interacting with a fluctuating number of pen pals. Though the Filipino postal system was a disaster, email made it possible to communicate with friends around the globe. After every furlough, my siblings and I returned to the Philippines with promises from new and old friends that they would write, and we hoped that somehow our bonds would transcend the distance. Few of those promises endured.

Then I began to email a missionary girl, Elizabeth, whom I knew from a previous Annual Field Conference. When we'd originally met, she was on the cusp of womanhood, with a boyish haircut that did injustice to the curves beginning to manifest. After the conference, several of the teens exchanged email addresses.

Elizabeth's mother was a Caucasian American and her father a Filipino. By the very nature of her existence, she seemed to intrinsically understand the conflict I felt between American and Filipino. On a superficial level, I belonged in two places, but on an internal level, I was an alien. Like me, Elizabeth spoke two languages, spent every fifth year on furlough, and didn't know which country to call home. If I couldn't belong in a place, it made sense to belong with a person.

Inevitably, Elizabeth and I developed reciprocal crushes. She was stateside for furlough, and the year she returned, we agreed to reunite at the Annual Field Conference in the fall. I can still picture the moment that I saw her again; it was dusk with the sun sinking in the distance. We met in a gazebo, away from prying eyes. Her hair was long now and spilled onto her shoulders in glossy black strands that shimmered with tinges of red in the setting sun. She smiled shyly, appearing young yet womanly all at the same time. I was enchanted.

We spent the week together, met each others' families, made eyes at each other, and communicated terribly with words. We schemed about how we could end up in the same school; I was going to ask my parents if I could attend her boarding school. The entire week built to a crescendo when I kissed her—my first kiss—an hour before saying goodbye and boarding the boat leaving Caliraya.

Once my family was on the road, my parents told my siblings and me that we were moving back to the U.S. I was stunned. I spent the day's car ride back to Naga City texting Elizabeth, telling her the horrible news. I wanted to cry but loathed the scrutiny that such an action would have brought from my siblings. I held myself together instead; being a missionary kid, I knew how to pretend.

My relationship with Elizabeth started to crumble almost immediately, though I was determined to make our relationship work. I'd kissed her, which was symbolic to me; I was committed, no matter the challenges. For my part, I was ready to plan a reunion with Elizabeth in college, four years later, where we would finally be together.

That sentiment wasn't reciprocated. Elizabeth started doubting our future almost immediately, or rather I suspect the new challenge accentuated doubts that she already had, doubts she hadn't shared before. She withdrew, bit by bit. I overcompensated, trying even harder to make the relationship work. My texts and emails became more frequent, hers less and less. I refused to give up gracefully, but the relationship was over long before I accepted reality.

At the time, my sister, Anna, was already married and living in the U.S. I remember one phone call with her where she talked about the family moving back to Kansas; she was excited to have the family close again. She must have heard the depression in my voice though because she made me promise not to do anything rash. As for Elizabeth, I believe she married the next guy she dated, another missionary boy who also attended field conference that year.

The final move back to the United States was staggering. For almost two decades, my family had been able to place our belongings in storage or have a friend house-sit during furloughs. All of the sudden, we had to pack eighteen years of accumulated personal effects, not the least of which was an extensive book collection that filled nine bookcases. The amount of clothing, toys, sports gear, school supplies, kitchen ware, videos, cassettes, televisions, computers, and other electronics required to raise and educate a family of eleven was overwhelming.

My parents had to decide what to keep and how to ship it to the other side of the globe, whether that meant sending it by boat in metal drums or bringing it as checked luggage on our return flight. They guessed at what we might immediately need upon our arrival. We gave our dogs away, sold our van, car, and motorcycle, guaranteed that our paperwork was in order, ended the lease on our house, and closed bank accounts. It was almost like dying—it was the end of a life after all—except the dead don't sort their own possessions. That work is left for others. We also needed a place to stay once we returned stateside. The process took months, and my mother only got through it all by praying and focusing on one day at a time.

Finally, we said goodbye to our friends in Naga City. The trip to Manila was less arduous than it was years before; the weaving roads still induced vomiting, but they were smoother now and the drive was nostalgic. Once we arrived at the mission house in the capital, we waited for the last few weeks, thinking that this might be the last time any of us ever studied the smoggy horizon lanced with skyscrapers and billboards. We knew this was the last time we'd order from Pizza Hut using a phone number that started with the digits 9-1-1, but that we'd instead soon be in the city where the pizza chain started. The days dragged by as slowly as the Manila traffic, yet we were sorry to see the time go.

During this last stay in Manila, we spent a day touring Corregidor Island. Because of its location at the entrance to Manila Bay, the island was outfitted with a network of tunnels and coastal artillery in order to protect the capital city. During World War II, Corregidor was the last bastion for American and some Filipino troops, and it was key to the liberation of the Philippines near the end of the war. The battles left the island in ruins.

My family traveled to the island by banka, the ocean waves lapping against the sides of the outrigger boat. The environment was lush and beautiful, with the island and coastlines separated by great spans of water, but as we drew closer to Corregidor's shores, I was struck by the trash floating in the waves that had collected against the docks. The scene was almost indicative of the Philippines: Natural splendor mixed with development, some of it careless. Wealth and poverty juxtaposed; hotels in slums where those in the high-rise can peer down upon those living in cardboard boxes.

We roamed among the remaining artillery. During the war, the paint peeled off many of the cannons due to the intense heat of incessant barrages, but they were all painted moss green now. We were surrounded by jungle vegetation, though the island had been mostly barren after years of explosions. The Malinta Tunnel, partly destroyed by the Japanese, was restored and housed a cinematic recreation of the battles. We toured the museums and memorials, wandering among statues and studying ruined buildings. Afterward, the boat ride back was an enjoyable yet melancholy affair, perhaps because of thoughts about the war, perhaps because our time in the Philippines was running out.

The morning of our departure transpired in the same fashion as past furloughs. Dad woke us up in the shadowy hours of the morning to a pile of suitcases and boxes that we loaded into taxis. The streets of Manila were empty and quiet, as if the city was dejected and sulking about the desertion. It was all familiar, the sleep-addled haze, the stinging eyes, the lines at the airport that curled around the inside of the building like pythons. This was our final exodus.

The building was filled with memories. It was in this very airport on a previous trip that Mom had trouble with her passport because she'd lost weight since the picture was taken. "Is that really you?" the check-in clerk wanted to know. She brought one of her coworkers over for a second opinion.

"Yes, that's her," the second clerk answered. "She's just sexy now."

The comment might have offended many Americans, but now Mom understood—to a Filipino, the words "sexy" and "attractive" are interchangeable. So many years later, the story seemed more amusing than before.

We waded through check-in, where we dropped off hundreds of pounds of luggage, and plodded through the customs stations. The lines and paperwork were bittersweet. We studied the details of the Manila airport one last time, from the glossy tile floor in the lobby to the carpeted hallways lit with fluorescent bulbs to the waiting room with a Duncan Donut shop. All too soon, we boarded an airplane. Moments later, we were taxiing along the runway and tossed into the air with the metropolis sprawling below us like a coral reef or a cluster of termite hills. Then we were surrounded by clouds, or perhaps it was smog. Before long, people slid the windows shut, and reality crept in: we had left our tropical home for the last time.

The rest of the journey passed peacefully enough. I believe it was during this trip that my parents got separated from Esther and a few of the other children in the Osaka airport in Japan. After two decades of foreign travel, Dad and Mom didn't panic; they waited serenely at the departure gate for the kids to show up, and they did.

Just as my family was incomplete when we arrived in the Philippines, so only a partial group of us returned together to the U.S.A.—Anna, Caleb, and Enoch were already stateside. There were no crying babies to coddle, no toddlers to explain the situation to. As the youngest, Hosanna was eight years old. The move was a mystery, even a shock, but there was none of the residual fairytale magic. This wasn't a dream or some temporary furlough. This was reality.

I can still picture arriving in Wichita, Kansas for the last time. The sky was crisp and blue and almost painfully bright, yet despite the sun, the outdoors somehow managed to appear cold. We taxied from the runway to the terminal, nosed into the exit ramp, and then silence. When the stewardess came on over the

P.A. system and told us to leave, some of us were lethargic, like reptiles waking from a stupor, numbed by lack of sleep, confused by the sunshine when our bodies murmured that it should be night.

We staggered down the jetway to where friends and relatives crowded together. The air in the building was cool and dry, dehydrating really, stripping the epidermis of moisture, drying mouths and stinging eyes. Suddenly we were in their midst of people, inundated in white skin and English, immersed in a cacophony where we somehow understood every syllable. In the midst of the hugs and strange pale faces, some of us stood there numb and wondering: What had we gotten ourselves into?

Foreigner: To Normal and Back Again

Before we left the Wichita airport, it became apparent that some cultural adjustment needed to be made. To start with, people at the airport were sitting on the floor. Filipinos never sit on the floor, as they consider it dirty; instead Filipinos squat. Also, at some point, Mom commented that she didn't remember where she had packed her thongs. Enoch turned to my mother and said, "Mom, we don't say 'thongs' in America. They aren't thongs; they're called 'flip-flops.' Thongs are something totally different."

To some of my younger siblings, our home country was relatively unknown. On one occasion, Nathan asked my father, "Are there McDonalds in America?" Likewise when we arrived stateside, Hosanna came out of the restroom exclaiming, "They have hot water [coming out of the faucet] here."

How were we supposed to call this strange place, with its pristine lawns and dainty fences, home? We were used to concrete and barbed wire and rice paddies. After childhoods spent in neighborhoods with buildings squeezed together and people living in stifling proximity to each other, the sweeping Kansas plains, crystal skies, and litter-free cities were ethereal, frightening even. There was more open space than we knew how to handle.

Having a birth certificate does not guarantee that your homeland is a place of rest. Third culture kids, individuals who grow up in more than one country, tend to feel homeless. In the Philippines, my siblings and I had familiar roles in society, but those roles were built around being different: We were the Americanos who could not blend in by nature of our skin color alone. Yet aspects of Filipino culture were grafted into our persons: we raised our eyebrows in greeting, ducked our heads when passing between strangers, and used our lips to point.

In America, all that was different. Suddenly we were invisible; no one starred at us when we walked down the street. Strangers weren't eager to strike up conversations. People weren't lining up for the chance to be our friends—admittedly, the application and interview process was probably too much. Being inconspicuous did not make us feel like we fit in either. It made us more aware that we didn't belong. We didn't understand aspects of American youth, like prom or pop culture. We couldn't identify famous actors or professional athletes; I'd never even seen Michael Jordan play basketball.

Suddenly my siblings and I had to learn the two great American sports—baseball and football—which we struggled to comprehend. In the Philippines, sports like basketball and tennis were popular because they did not demand large amounts of land, and the courts were useful for drying rice during harvest time. Baseball and football require vast spaces and were simply impractical alternatives in a small island country.

Football was especially confusing to me even as an older teenager. Why did the game start and stop with such frequency? Was it just for the sake of commercials? Often enough they were more entertaining than the game. Were the goal posts purely aesthetic? There seemed to be something odd about guys watching a bunch of muscular men run around in spandex. Did the camera need to focus on their posteriors so much? Perhaps the biggest questions were where in the world the yellow line came from, how it was able to appear and disappear, and why the referees always felt the need to check if it was right or not? Could they not see it? Were they blind? That certainly seemed to be the popular opinion.

My experience of football was not limited to the television; it spilled into the backyard. I discovered that I enjoyed tackling people, even though I was a scrawny kid and many of my athletic ventures ended poorly. There was one particular day in high school when I picked myself off the ground with the question, "How am I ever going to live this down?" skittering through my scattered thoughts.

All I remembered was that I had the football, that I was sprinting along the edge of our backyard field, and that Taylor, a freshman girl, was standing several yards in front of me. I remembered thinking, rather egotistically, "No problem," as I closed the gap and feeling rather bad that I was going to hit a girl. Still she chose to play.

Suddenly I was on the ground. I was not sure how that had happened. All my friends were laughing. Why were my friends laughing? And why was I on the ground? Taylor stood several feet off looking guilty. Why were my friends laughing? This was not funny. Even then I knew that there must have been a law imbedded somewhere in American man code stating, "Thou shall not get flattened by females while playing football." At least I hadn't fumbled.

America was also full of rules I had to get my head around. There were the obvious aspects, like traffic regulations. With the multitude of signs, it took months for me to understand what they all meant. Even the lines down the middle of the road had different meanings. There were regulations about polluting, cutting grass, and trimming trees. I even heard about a bizarre curfew law in our town, which meant I couldn't be out later than a certain hour at night.

Perhaps most confusing of all to me were the myriad of laws tied to the Fish and Game Department. To hunt in Kansas, you had to take a hunter safety course. Then you had to buy a hunting license, special stamps to hunt certain animals, and tags for deer and turkeys. You could only shoot a regimented number of a specific species of animal with regulated kinds of guns and ammunition within specifics hours of the day during special days of the years. It was also necessary to buy a new license each year.

Fishing was almost as complicated. You needed a license, but depending on which license you bought you could only use one, two, or three fishing poles. Only certain techniques were legal—no nets, no snagging. Once you caught a fish, it had to be a certain size based on its species, or you had to let it go. In the Philippines, if you caught a fish, you ate it—without worrying about water quality or mercury levels. Naturally, many of these laws varied from state to state, but there wasn't a law guidebook at each state boundary.

Fitting into this new culture was its own struggle. I recall a particular conversation I had with a friend, Kody, one furlough, a couple years before my family left the mission field. We were in middle school and discussing the girls in the church middle school group, particularly the ones we wanted to date. There was one girl I liked in particular; she was about my age, curvy, and dark eyed—of course, I knew nothing about her personality because I was a kid and too superficial to think about such things. Kody confided in me that he had talked with her about me. All she had to say is that she thought I was weird—I assumed because I was a missionary kid. Years later, I hadn't forgotten.

For each of my siblings the process of carving out a niche in America looked different. For instance, Anna married another former missionary kid while Enoch moved to Canada and married a Canadian. Meanwhile, some of my younger siblings seemed able to join American culture easily enough because of their age; they were young enough that they didn't have to abandon an identity to fit. As far as I could tell, they simply adjusted to a new one.

For my part, I became obsessed with blending into American teenage life. The last thing I wanted was to be the weird kid who grew up in the Philippines and who nobody wanted to befriend or date. For kids and teenagers being popular is all about assimilation. Though I wasn't attending a public school, that same principle still applied to my interactions with my new peers. In order to fit in, I castigated my past life. I did not bring up my experiences abroad or meditate on my prior life within my peer group; I embraced the new culture, my new home culture. After being poked and stared at and a topic of conversation, I fixated on normalcy. Hiding my experience abroad and home school background became a point of pride. However, by sequestering the past, I lost one of the central elements of myself, as people often do when they attempt to conform to society or what they believe society desires. It was years before I recognized what I'd lost.

In the meantime, one problem troubled me more than any other. All my life Filipino girls had thrown themselves at me because I was an American and therefore perceived as mature, rich, and handsome. When I returned to Kansas, girls ignored me. I had to wonder what was wrong with them: didn't they realize I was special? I was practically famous.

Then reality struck: I was average height, weighed one hundred and fifteen pounds on a good day, and wore glasses. I wasn't particularly athletic or physically striking. I wasn't really sure what puberty was, at least not from personal experience. The only edge I had was a quick wit and a dry sense of humor.

Along with my girl problems, I couldn't understand the fascination among my new friends with being able to drive. The Midwestern teenager's quest for a driver's license was a mystery. When I was growing up, I could get in a jeepney or tricycle and commute without accruing the expenses of gasoline, mechanical repairs, and insurance. As young teenagers, my brothers and I spent many of our afternoons venturing to the internet cafes in downtown Naga City, rooms stuffed full of computers and students. We'd hangout for hours, the only light coming from computer monitors. The air filled with the noise of keyboards and mice clicking, sounds effects from video games, and the banter of patrons as they challenged each other in cyber realms. It was one of my favorite pastimes, one I didn't need a car to enjoy. Still, society was different in America.

For my new peers without a cheap public transportation option, the learner's permit at fifteen and the driver's license at sixteen were gateways to freedom and independence, the price offset by new possibilities, such as jobs and dating freedoms. However, my path to automotive autonomy was delayed several years. My family moved back stateside when I was around seventeen, but I could not drive in the Philippines until I was eighteen. As I result, I was behind from the start; I was seventeen before I secured my learner's permit and eighteen before I got my license. Even then, it was years before I grudgingly accepted the responsibility of owning and maintaining a vehicle of my own.

As I attempted to escape or ignore my past, its influences were everywhere. I emphasized fitting in, building relationships, and being popular in my remaining high school years only to then graduate. My friends left for new academic endeavors. Still, I reset for junior college. I made new friends, and for a couple years, things were normal. Then I graduated with my Associates degree. This time, I left Wichita.

Only at my new university did I stop trying so hard to build new relationships. After years of making new friends and losing them, I was sick of the effort and the loss. By this point, even my siblings were leaving home. I couldn't see the point to trying to build again, only to leave in two more years. Finally, I just stopped trying to fit in, to be likeable, and to belong. I just was. Though I was making nearly perfect grades, I was easy to miss in a classroom or a college club; I was one of the people who said the least and who left the party early—not because I was intimidated, but because I was tired of the cycle.

It was my creative writing instructors in college who convinced me to return to my roots through my writing. When they found out about my experiences abroad, they invariably encouraged me to share them. For the most part while I was in college, I refused, focusing instead on stories or essays that were more traditionally American. If someone read my story and accepted it as normal, they were, by extension, accepting my ability to match the culture.

At the same time, I started to understand that life in the college environment wasn't about assimilation anymore. In a college like the University of Kansas where there were 30,000 students, being weird wasn't particularly negative; there were already enough strange people around that it was quite possible to find an equally strange peer group. Popularity wasn't based purely on traits like athleticism. My background suddenly had value.

It was during my senior year and afterward that I began to meditate on my seventeen years as a missionary kid, years I had ignored. I wrote, and I processed and reflected as I wrote. In reliving and analyzing the past, I became whole again. I started to appreciate my experiences, who I was, and why I think and perceive and respond slightly askance. I began to share the tales of my childhood with friends or groups of people at social gatherings, tales they found immensely entertaining.

Then I understood that I was a talented storyteller beginning to come into my own. There was solace in the contemplation and the acceptance that I wasn't normal, that being weird was okay. I had a perspective that no one else could replicate. As I accepted that perspective, I recognized it for what it is: a gift.

Thoughts on Unicorns

I've heard it said that virgins are like unicorns, meaning that they are rare, bordering on fantasy, and that saving sex for marriage is naïve and childish. Many hold that unicorns are prudes. Have been raised in a large, conservative family I can understand this to a degree: we tend to avoid situations that would endanger our mythological status until after our wedding. Regrettably, there are also plenty of people in church history who treated sex as if it were dirty, undesirable or accidental, which blatantly contradicts Scriptures like Song of Solomon.

Growing up I encountered many churchgoers who treated sex as if it is some dark, secret topic. Just a few Sundays ago, I was in church speaking with one of the pastors after the service, and I mentioned the words "sperm" and "eggs," in scandalously close proximity in my sentence. Immediately a lady several rows ahead turned around and starred at me, as if she worried that my sentence was in danger of impregnating itself. Her expression read: "This is church; we don't discuss such things here." I for one was not aware that God didn't create sperm and eggs, or that in Genesis 1:31 on the sixth day when He "saw all that he had made, and it was very good" that God was considering everything other than sex.

Large families, mine included, rarely come into existence without a vigorous sex life; this should be axiomatic, yet somehow people manage to forget. It can be surprising how frequently and candidly sex is a topic of discourse among my siblings, though generally not in public—at least not without whispers or coded terminology. Over the years, it is as if the boys in the family—okay mostly me—made it our duty to help our sisters understand the male mentality toward sex while the girls in the family decided to help their brothers comprehend the female sexual mindset. The guys have emphasized the physical needs and the girls the emotional needs. As a result, both the male and the female unicorn populations in my family are better equipped to have fulfilling post-unicorn existences in the future.

There's an understanding amongst us that sex can be funny, and that it's wholesome to joke and laugh about it in a manner that isn't demeaning. Just the other day, I was at Anna and her husband's house. The three of us were sitting on the living room floor, chatting in front of the fireplace. David got up to check on the kids, and as soon as he walked out the door, Anna loudly announced, "So about Sex 101." Predictably, David reappeared back in the doorway, a grin on his face, the errand no longer important.

My siblings haven't always been so open in our discussions. I still remember the moment, almost a decade ago, that opened the floodgates. It was the day Anna and David got married. After the wedding, they stopped by my parents' house to drop off a friend's suitcase before they left for their honeymoon, and there was a smattering of people in the living room. About fifteen years old at the time, I sent one glance in the newlyweds' direction and announced, "Well, her hair still looks nice. Nothing exciting has happened yet." Anna turned crimson, but after that experience, my siblings were notably less inhibited in their conversations.

Even before I broke the spoken boundary around sex, my family members all understood that sex had a frequent and flourishing place in our home within my parents' relationship. When it came to the master bedroom and my father's office, there was a specific entrance policy. If there was a large hair twisty around the doorknob, it meant that they could not be disturbed, except in the direst circumstances. If they were interrupted for anything that was not life or death, the situation would swiftly become such. While the twisty could also warn of an important phone call or a marital adjustment, it was well understood that international calls were expensive, my parents rarely fought, and that most of the time the twisty meant "See you in the morning."

There were other telltale signs as well: If the next day the light bulbs in all their lamps were colored instead of plain old incandescent bulbs, we knew what had happened. To this day, we realize why Dad and Mom schedule the remaining kids to be out of the house on Wednesday afternoons—surprise, Mom and Dad: yes, we know what that's about.

It's not like my parents have tried to hide the joys of a healthy sexual relationship. One year when my family was on furlough, Dad was accosted by a man who said about our family size, "Mr. Gray, you do know what causes that, don't you?"

My father smiled back and answered, "Yes. And it sure was fun."

This same mentality has transferred to us kids. A few years ago, I was at Anna and David's house with a few of my siblings. Abigail went to use the master bathroom, and she came back rather embarrassed. After several questions, Anna realized what Abby was blushing about: Anna had left a note for David on the mirror and forgot to erase it before her siblings arrived. It read, "So you wanna?"

Given all this, the question becomes, "Why wait?" If my siblings and I have such high opinions of sexual intimacy, why prolong unicorn status? Admonitions in the Bible to keep the marriage bed pure are not there to indicate that sex is an evil thing. God didn't create Adam and Eve, return the next day, and go, "Wait, hold on a minute. You put what where? That's so gross. I never saw that coming." There was design and intent, and it was very good. However, because there was design and intent, there was also a plan for sex so that it could be enjoyed fully and protected: that "a man leaves his father and mother and is united to his wife, and they become one flesh," as it is phrased in Genesis 2:24. In these parameters, sex can flourish to its fullest extent with a sense of safety that can last a lifetime.

At twenty-five, I'm still a unicorn—yes, sometimes people ask for my autograph—but I'm not still a virgin because I haven't had opportunities or because I don't have sexual desires; I, like many of my siblings, made a choice years ago that I would wait. It's rarely been easy. There are mornings and evenings, sometimes entire days, where standing firm and sticking with the decision not to have sex before marriage is awful. Commitment to keeping the marriage bed pure isn't as simple as not having intercourse; it means watching what you meditate on and what you communicate and the situations you place yourself in—though I'd be lying if I said I hadn't made innumerable mistakes along the way. Some days this commitment means resisting the deepest urges of biology, even though it's hard when you want nothing more than the intimate touch of another. It means loving someone yet choosing to go to sleep alone every night and wake in isolation every morning for a little bit longer.

Why? Why put off the gratification, the intimacy? I think there are several reasons—probably more than I can consciously understand and express. One of the chief reasons is security. Knowing that my future wife had the discipline and self-control to wait over a decade or decades enables me to feel a deeper level of trust. In my search for a marriage partner, I've realized that a woman who held the line sexually in the past is much more likely to hold the line in the future when the marriage isn't easy, during sickness or financial crisis or any number of other events, when infidelity or divorce appear to be easier paths.

A friend once confided in me that she had contracted H.P.V., and the disease placed her at high risk of developing cervical cancer and threatened her ability to have children. The acuteness of her pain and depression was evidenced by the brevity of her words as she shared. This was a friend whom I had cautioned about premarital sex. Yet as I absorbed her words, I had no desire to condemn her past decisions, no desire to remind her that I had warned her. I wanted to comfort her, to alleviate her suffering, to erase the past, and I knew that God felt the same—hence the repeated admonitions in the Bible to wait.

Babies are of course another factor to consider. The reality is that, from a biological standpoint, when unicorns stop being unicorns, there's a chance that new unicorns will magically appear. Few forms of birth control can completely separate sex from the possibility of conception. My family is no exception; a significant number of pregnancies—both children and grandchildren—occurred despite attempted birth control. The prospect of creating life is no small responsibility, and no infant should enter the world undesired or uncared for. The simplest way for me to protect my children's futures is for me to live with self-control.

There's also the issue of emotional scarring. Every one of my past romantic relationships has left scars that I have to deal with as I live now, but the damage has been restricted because those relationships failed before there was sexual intimacy. As a result, I will be able to enter marriage as a more whole person. The promise of secure, wholistic sex in the future is alluring.

I cannot adequately express my excitement for the day when I do finally have sex. It'll be awkward and amusing and probably pretty graceless. Still, it'll be with my best friend, and we'll have the rest of our lives to figure it out. When we're spent, we won't have to worry about whether the other person loves us or if we're right for each other or if we'll get married; those questions will all have been answered already, the covenant made. So I wait.

In all this, I remember that in many ways the reason I can imagine and anticipate such a future with confidence is because my parents have modeled a healthy sexual relationship. I know that it's for real and worth the cost, not some fantasy concocted by clergymen to restrict the amusement of their congregation. A few years ago, after most of my siblings were living away from home, Josiah, Abby and Hosanna came home from school. When they arrived, there was a note taped to the door with a twenty dollar bill. The message said, in essence, "Go out to dinner for a few hours. Then you can come home." At that time, my parents had been married for over thirty years. Stories like these remind me that being a unicorn is worthwhile.

Number Four

For my family there are no flawless family photos; someone has his eyes closed, or someone else's smile is actually a smirk, or one sibling is pinching or elbowing another, or maybe we're all just sick of posturing. Perfect doesn't exist. It would be superficial to claim that I have always loved being a member of a family of eleven. That simply is not true. Sometimes I've disliked being one of nine kids. When I was a teenager, people would discover that I had four brothers and four sisters, and they would inquire where in the sequence I fell out.[6] I'd respond, "I'm number four; in other words, obsolete."

I was a jaded, angst-ridden teenager, though I was not as blatant with my irritation as others. Caleb and Enoch both rebelled in more visible fashions, sometimes challenging parental authority without much reservation. In contrast, I lived by the mantra, "What my parents don't know can't hurt me." Perhaps I wasn't overtly rebellious, but I had my moments.

---

[6] Of course when you've had nine kids the later births aren't really births at all; the child simply waltzes out of the birth canal, clean as a whistle, fully potty trained, and asks, "Which bunk is mine?"

One Sunday when my family was in the United States, I was sitting in a service with the rest of the church high school group. The pastor was preaching a sermon that somehow touched on stereotypes, and he proceeded to list several, saying something like, "All blonds are ditzy, white people can't jump, all parents are out of touch..."

At this last point I hollered from the back of the sanctuary, "Amen."

I quickly realized that I had spoken too soon as the pastor went on to finish, "And all teenagers are rebellious."

All around the auditorium parents answered back, "Amen."

There was some basis to my resentment, though much of it was rather silly. I tired of hand-me-downs, I normally had to share a room, and having such a large family meant I had plenty of chores. Most strikingly, I didn't feel like I knew my father when I was growing up. When I was a child, in a lot of ways Dad was kind of like God in that he was a looming authority figure, except Dad felt less approachable.

Much of the time when I interacted with my father in a one-on-one setting, it was because I had been horrid enough that Mom didn't feel like she could provide a sufficient reprimand. Unlike my mother, my father was rarely passionate and not easily affected by emotions or circumstance. We'd sit in his office, which was lined with shelves of books, videos, and cassette tapes, while he'd patiently listen to Mom's indictments. Then she would leave. I'd be left alone with Dad and given a chance to explain myself before he gave a verdict.

His calm was disconcerting to me, the silence more imposing than any word or emotional response could have been. When he spoke, he did so slowly; when he disciplined, it was with such marked resignation that it was clear he took no joy in punishment. The worst part was simply being the focus of his consternation.

However, this scenario made up most of the one-on-one time I remember getting with my father at a young age; I had little frame of reference for viewing him as anything other than an authority figure.

Doubtless to many of my siblings, this sense of distance wasn't quite the same because they knew my father better than I did. My sense that my father was a stranger was likely accentuated both by my place in the family birth order and by the point in my parents' lives when I was born. My father simply could not give me, as the fourth child, the same degree of attention that Anna, Caleb, and Enoch received—as they say, "After three children you're playing zone defense." Likewise, my being born shortly after the family moved to the Philippines meant my father was especially caught up in all the new responsibilities accompaning the transition.

It's also true that the more vocal kids monopolized my parents' time; in life, the loudest problems are the ones that get addressed first. Caleb, Enoch, and Nathan competed for inventive or more severe punishments. Not long ago I was driving with Nathan and Josiah when Nathan confessed, "Sometimes when we were little, I'd beat on Josiah just so I'd get in trouble and get time with Dad." Turning to Josiah, he added, "Sorry, Siah."

Other family members, like Esther, were more likely to assume the spotlight if they had a question or concern, but I simply did not have a personality that lent itself to requesting attention. Dad fondly recounts how Esther once, as a child, was reading 1 Timothy 2:12 and discovered where Paul says, "I do not permit a woman to teach or to assume authority over a man." Esther rushed to my father's office and demanded, "What is this?" Dad dropped what he was doing and had an extensive conversation with Esther about biblical womanhood.

At the same time, in life I often find myself searching not for answers to my problems but for sympathy in them—a trait that I am ruefully aware is generally attributed to women. I want to solve my own problems, but both of my parents are solution-oriented people. If I went to them with an issue, they would try to fix it, so I learned to go to Anna for sympathy instead.

That is not to say I never got time with Dad as I aged. On a couple of our furlough years as a teenager, I was able to spend days hunting with my father and some of my siblings, an experience I enjoyed. We hunted a variety of wildlife: quail, pheasant, ducks, and deer. We'd rise early in the morning to march through fields, sneak up on ponds, or wait in ambush in tree stands. The memories are pleasant, and I hunt to this day as a result of those experiences.

I also spent a number of my Saturday mornings biking with Dad when I was in high school. Biking in the Philippines, like crossing the street, is an extreme sport. The only constant rule of the road is that the largest vehicle has the right away, regardless of who is in which lane. My dad tells the story of how he was once driving our van along the highway when, suddenly, he spotted a bus speeding straight toward him, in my father's lane. The oncoming bus driver flashed his head lights and gestured at my father to get out of the way, which he did, and if my father had not complied there would have been a head-on collision.

On another occasion while biking, a motorcycle pulled out directly in front of my father, who was coasting down this mountain road and did not have enough time to brake. Dad swerved and narrowly missed the motorcycle, but this forced him onto a driveway that was bordered on its sides with a three-inch lip and then a two-foot drop off. Unable to stop, my dad hopped the front wheel of his bike over the lip, but the rear wheel hit, flipping the bike up and toward my father. He crashed to the ground with the bike on top of him. Despite the danger, the biking did allow my father to get some cardio exercise and build relationships with local businessmen, as many of them were avid bikers.

I often joined my dad on the road, not because I enjoyed the experience, but because Mom insisted that I spend time with him. Truth be told, I hated the majority of the experience. We'd start biking early in the morning in order to beat at least some of the heat. We pedaled along our narrow highway, through a neighborhood or two, all the while weaving between pedestrians and tricycles and bicycles with sidecars, until we reached another highway. Meanwhile, jeepneys and cars blew past us at hazardous speeds.

The route we took went about fifteen kilometers, ending part way up a mountain where we rested before turning home. Being together meant biking side-by-side or in a line, while perspiring profusely, and talking meant less oxygen for exertion. Much of the scenery around us was impressive, lush fields and rice paddies with mountains in the distance or straight ahead, but much of the time I didn't notice. I struggled to keep up and almost always finished the rides several minutes behind.

I spent much of the trips in my head, wishing I could sleep in. Certainly, I was spending time with my father, but I did not feel that he got to know me any better in the process. There was always a part of my mind complaining that spending time with Dad usually meant joining whatever activity he was already doing. I felt like a number dragged along for the sake of convenience; I might as well have been Caleb or Enoch or Nathan or Josiah—they would have performed just as well—I was simply the right age and available.

The first time I remember feeling distinct in my father's mind was during the summer between graduating high school and starting junior college. We'd been back in the U.S. for a while, and for the last few years my family had traveled out to Colorado to trout fish. However, this particular year there were scheduling difficulties, so my father and I, the two aggressive fishermen in the family, went on our own.

The trip lasted about a week. We woke up in the mornings, just Dad and me, and drove to the chain of ponds that stair-stepped their way down pine-studded mountains. The mornings were sheathed in mist; the days in sunshine and tranquility. I caught almost twice as many trout as Dad did, though he caught several that were larger, until the last day of the week when I caught our record. It was a rainbow trout that I had hooked twice the day before but lost each time; then I hooked it again that last, final day on a lure my grandfather owned. After a skirmish that shattered the surface of the pond, the trout lay on the shore. I was ecstatic.

Still, not all that week was about the beauty of mountains and meadows; I had a secret, a confession to make. I had entered my teenage years as the pornographic industry discovered a brand new channel: the internet. Suddenly, pop-up advertisements magically appeared on browsers, and people got lascivious invitations in their email. Few Christians, my parents included, knew how to respond; the technology was new, and spam boxes, internet filters, and accountability software weren't yet invented, or at least accessible.

As a young teenager, I didn't go looking for internet pornography. It found me, and then I learned how to look for it, starting with tamer temptations, like the Sports Illustrated Swimsuit Edition, and going on from there. I inherently knew that pornography was wrong, but I didn't tell anyone what I was doing. I was a missionary kid; I was supposed to know better and be above such sins—of course, I couldn't talk to anyone about it Instead, I lived in this addicted cycle where I'd resist for weeks or months before falling into a binge period.

When Dad and I went to Colorado, I was struggling aggressively yet again with my pornographic addiction, and I desperately wanted to tell him. I remember spending much of the week trying to muster my courage to confess and ask for help, but I simply couldn't do it. Even on the ride home, as our last few hours alone together expired, I couldn't form the words. Instead, I watched as the highway slipped away and the Rockies faded further out of sight. I was terrified of disappointing him.

For the longest time, I adamantly opposed to the idea of reproducing someday, largely because I knew that children were a lot of work. Eventually though, I gave in to the idea that I might perhaps someday have kids, if I couldn't possibly control myself. I insisted though that I would only have a few because I wanted to provide them with the individual attention that I did not feel like I had received at a young age and which I self-righteously felt I deserved. I clung to this mindset for years. It was not until college that my attitude shifted.

When I left home for the University of Kansas, several things happened. To begin with, I started handling my own bills more; I wasn't paying my tuition, living expenses, or food bill, but I was functioning in an intermediate role in which I incurred the bills, paid them temporarily, and brought them to my father for reimbursement. This let me see exactly how much money my parents were paying in order for me to get my college degree. Suddenly I began to recognize the value my parents placed on me; I had a list of paid expenses to prove it. Meanwhile, my relationship with my parents, particularly my father, began to change as they became advisors instead of authority figures.

I wasn't homesick when I left my family, but I grew homesick the longer I was away. At the start, I was very caught up in the independence of being away from home; I could eat what I wanted, sleep when I wanted, and I had control over my schedule. I had the increased academic challenge and KU basketball to keep up with. As the semesters rushed on, however, I started missing my family, from the deep conversations to the strong bonds to the freedom to be myself without fear of reproach. Before

I graduated, I started going home with increasing frequency; once I even drove the 366 mile round trip even though I only spent the night at home and returned the next day. Distance gave perspective. I realized my mother was right when she told us children as we were growing up that our deepest friendships would be within our own family.

Along with my new appreciation for my family, I recognized the impact that Enoch's leaving for boarding school had on me. With Anna and Caleb so much older, Nathan and Josiah partners in crime, and the three younger girls absorbed in imaginary adventures, it was logical that Enoch and I shared a special bond as children. We embodied the Filipino concept of pakikisama—togetherness—we were companions. We filled our time with slingshots and, when my parents were not watching, sword fights in which I would get hurt. Then Enoch would let me hit him back and feign mortal injury. When we played LEGOS, I would create a design that Enoch modified and expanded.

With Enoch's departure to Manila for school, my experience of pakikisama ended. I began playing by myself, spending hours alone in our sandbox with my army men or frequenting the internet cafes. During the school breaks, Enoch returned, but things were never like before. He didn't even go by Enoch anymore; he went by Nic—some missionary kids had started calling him Eunuch, so he decided a new nickname was necessary. He spent time with older and more mature kids now. He could name actors, had seen R-rated movies, and played with fire and knives when he thought Dad and Mom weren't watching. We had moments of pakikisama, but not like before, and they never lasted. Once I got to the University of Kansas, realization hit: I wasn't bitter about having a big family; I was bitter about losing my childhood friend. Having siblings afforded me that friendship in the first place.

Maybe most importantly of all, I observed Anna and her husband, David, as their family expanded from one child to five children. One conversation in particular still stands out to me.

We were talking about the response David frequently received when he announced to friends or coworkers that he and Anna were expecting their fifth child. Husbands would smirk at him and ask, "Don't you know what causes that?"

"I can't believe they think it's so witty, like they're the first person to say it," David snorted. "It's not funny at all. It's rude."

"I know what you should tell them." I told David. "You should look at them and say, 'Yes. I know what causes that. My wife just enjoys it more than yours does.'"

I continued to watch as Anna and David wrestled with the growth: Should they use birth control; were they trying to control their lives instead of relinquishing control to God; how would they provide financially or emotionally; would they have enough time? It was a struggle with a myriad of facets. They once prayed, as my mother did, that Anna wouldn't conceive for months, but Anna got pregnant almost immediately. There were other issues at play as well. For instance, some forms of oral birth control impacted Anna's mood, and there's the reality that sex with a condom, according to David, is like trying to eat frozen yogurt with a sock on your tongue or a slice of chocolate cake through a straw.

However, I noticed that my nephews and niece were different than other kids their age. They were still kids, but they were notably less selfish than their peers who had fewer brothers and sisters or none at all. Having multiple siblings meant that my nephews and niece were forced to realize that they were not the center of the universe, that they weren't entitled to special treatment.

This addresses one of the challenges that parents face: from birth, children are self-absorbed, naively aware only of themselves, and at first they see the problems and needs and feelings of others as important only because they can upset the balance of their childish world. It takes love and discipline for children to realize that their needs and desires are one small part of a global conscious. Parents are tasked with concurrently helping their children become more independent and less narcissistic.

Anna's children were more patient for their ages, grasped the importance of work, and viewed themselves as part of a family unit—all characteristics that will make them more constructive adults in society. When I reflected on my siblings, I realized that every single one of them who had reached adulthood was a vibrant part of his or her community.

At the same time, when I study my own generation in America, the dominant characteristic is entitlement; we feel that we deserve a college education, a job, a car, a house in the suburbs, and healthcare. Rather than being diligent and persistent in our efforts, we expect these privileges to materialize or be provided by a larger entity. I am grateful that I grew up in a family where I was forced to learn early on that I was valuable but that the world did not revolve around me. The size of my family is one of the great blessings of my life.

I noticed something else watching Anna and David. Raising kids is an amateur sport; parents don't know exactly what they're doing. There are no trial sessions, just flawed games with a myriad of mistakes. Watching the challenges my nephews and niece presented, I suddenly wanted to be more gracious with my parents. Certainly they bobbled some catches, but they also hit plenty of sacrificial fly balls, whether it was giving up time or finances or anything else. Besides, Dad and Mom likely did a better job parenting with nine kids than they would have with just four; having so many kids requires that you, as a parent or child, focus on your family.

And parents grow. It's easy to think as children that our parents are adults so they are these fully-developed, static characters in a story that is about us, the kids. The reality is that parents are still growing; they battle the same narcissistic tendencies that a child does, just on a different plateau. Children are simply in the earlier stages of development. The closer I get to fatherhood, the more I recognize that having kids is a part of growth. It's a part of growth that I want to delay or regulate because I'm selfish and afraid; I don't want to make the sacrifices that go along with parenthood. I like my time and my money and the freedom to do what I choose when I choose and how I choose. I want control of my world, and the thought of having kids forces me to recognize that my sense of control is an illusion. Instead of maturing to the point when I can say, "I'm not in control, but I'm going to do what I can to give myself to those around me," I like the idea of staying put.

At the same time, when I look at my country, what I realize is that having kids is a part of growing up. By refusing to have children or rejecting the idea of having more than a couple kids, Americans have become increasingly more childish themselves, to the extent that selfishness and entitlement are cultural characteristics. In order for a country to succeed, however, its people have to be able to see beyond themselves because no country is borne without sacrifice.

I can't speak from a place of experience in this area; I'm young, not some patriarch. I won't claim that I will never use birth control—in all fairness, that is a decision I have to make with my future wife. It's also worth mentioning that the Bible doesn't contain an explicit command to have as many children as possible. It's critical not to fall into legalism.

I haven't had frozen yogurt or chocolate cake yet, so it's hard to speak with authority. Still, in the spirit of reflection and contemplation I will say this: I believe all good parents want more for their kids than they themselves received from their parents. We want our children to be more whole than we are. If I'm honest with myself, I have to acknowledge that having lots of brothers and sisters is an enormous part of my completeness. I doubt I'll ever be able to settle for giving less.

Perfect

Missionary kids are normal kids but better actors. There's nothing new about the children of missionaries and pastors struggling with their place in the church. The jaded offspring of clergymen are everywhere: Katy Perry, Daniel Tosh, Alice Cooper—all wildly successful yet strikingly different from their religious upbringing. I would be amiss if I indicated that even my own thoughts about the church and being a missionary kid and even God are all of an amiable nature.

At the same time, it is also possible to attribute false causes to some of life's unfairness. For instance, it grieves me that my paternal grandmother, who worked as a librarian and saved for my college education, was never able to experience how passionate I am about literature and writing. I could blame this on growing up abroad and even say that my grandfather was right when he objected to my parents' plans to depart for the Philippines. But that would be a fallacious claim.

My grandmother was a fiercely independent feminist. As a part of her autonomous mentality, she smoked, regardless of what anybody else said. Before my father was born, Grandmother was quarantined with tuberculosis. Decades later, she contracted lung cancer, underwent chemotherapy, and caught pneumonia. She died years before my family returned stateside, and her death kept me from connecting with her. Nonetheless, I didn't fully discover—if indeed I have yet—my affinity for prose until years after my family returned to America. However, being a missionary kid did not come between my grandmother and me connecting over the English language.

Furthermore, if my parents had not left the U.S., I would not have experienced some of my life's great blessings. My parents likely would not have home schooled, in which case Mom probably would never have encountered Mary Pride's book, *The Way Home*, and I would be the family bookend—I would not have my youngest five siblings. That means many of the stories I have recounted would never have happened. Much of the inspiration for this book would not exist.

Allocating blame is a fickle and facetious business. I want to be transparent without casting victims and villains, and I may well fail in that endeavor. Still, I am obligated to try, though I may do so imperfectly.

I've spent most of my life in the church being watched. In some ways, this is natural and healthy; repeatedly, the New Testament stresses that those in leadership in the church should have families that are reputable. My actions growing up, whether good or bad, were a reflection on my father and had the potential to damage his career. Being born to an ordained minister of the gospel meant I was born in a spotlight, like I was the child of a lesser celebrity. Strangers knew my name and scrutinized my every step. Before I knew Jesus, I was expected to be like Him; I was immediately held to a standard of perfection I had no internal desire to pursue.

There were times when other parents held me, a missionary kid, as the standard which their children were to attain. They were to possess my manners, my poise, and my fervor. But often those attributes felt like a mask that I donned as a part of my Christian performance. I was a perfect piece in a perfect family, a pawn in an ivory chess set. Only I wasn't ivory all the way through; I wasn't even close, and I knew it.

When I was in middle school, I remember standing outside one of our supporting churches with a friend. A couple of middle school girls darted past, engaged in animated conversation. One of the girls was irate and swore as she was going by. My friend turned to me and said, "I want to smack her. Doesn't she have any respect for God's house?"

Though I didn't say anything, I was grieved by my friend's comment. Hadn't Jesus said something like, "Out of the overflow of the heart the mouth speaks"? I took this to mean that, when people behaved poorly, we should be less concerned about their actions and more concerned about whatever was causing the problem inside. How could we ever expect to become better Christians if we never gave vent to our struggles and begrudged others' honesty?

Still, my friend's words stayed with me.

For much of my childhood, the discrepancy between my public actions and my private life didn't bother me very much. What others didn't know couldn't hurt me, I reasoned. Long before I was a teenager, I could, and often did, out-swear most children my age, though only a few of my brothers knew. And as I grew older, there was no safe way to talk about issues like temptation, lust, and pornography on a personal level. I felt alone as I began to experience the temptations common to man. In the midst of the dichotomy of who I was and who I was supposed to be, it was impossible to find sanctuary in the church. To this day, I consider Saturday more of a Sabbath than Sunday because, to me, attending church is work.

It would be an oversimplification to say that I was always a wayward child; it also wouldn't be true. I was only three years old when I accepted Jesus' sacrifice as the way I could be reconciled to God. My excitement was such that I quickly informed my best friend, Evan, who responded, "I want to do that too." I had a similar experience when I was four. I was perched atop a jeep with a Filipino named Jun as we watched a projection of the Jesus film in a field. Throughout the movie, I jabbered incessantly about Jesus. Jun was so intrigued that he talked with my dad afterward, asking to know more about Jesus, and finally surrendered his life to God. Moments like this, though rarely happening to this extreme, continued to occur as I aged.

Still I was overshadowed by awareness that I wasn't who I ought to be. Living in deception is one of the most exhaustive ways of life. As I passed through my teenage years and into adulthood, my trepidation built. I couldn't be honest, I couldn't be authentic, and I was living within the church as a stranger.

In my experience, the Christ-like behavior of those who call themselves Christians tends to fall into a spectrum made up of three lenses: being, performing, or acting. Being is the first lens, the simplest form of existence. For a person who is simply being, actions flow directly out of innate desires without being tweaked or channeled or disguised. In a childlike manner, they simply exist. When I shared my faith with Evan and Jun, it wasn't because I was compelled from the outside but by something within me. I acted like a believer in Christ purely because I believed.

The second lens, performing, is slightly different and more complex. A juggler is still a juggler regardless of whether or not he is juggling. Nevertheless, there are points when he puts on a performance by juggling, though there is no deception. He is simply on his best behavior. When I mingled with the laity at missions conferences and distributed clipboards and post cards, my behavior wasn't facetious; I was just on my best behavior, performing based on my identity.

Acting, the final lens, resides on the far end of the spectrum. Actors don the guise of their character for a time, temporarily becoming someone they're not. They can change from skin to skin, become hero, villain, or victim. Their actions often move independently of their internal identity. Christians who move into this lens live in fear of the truth lest they be discovered by their peers; their attention is focused on men rather than God who perceives the truth of all things.

The border between these lenses can be almost imperceptible. And an outsider, in order to glimpse being, has to peer through performing and acting.

Ideally, a clergyman exists solely in the first category. Nonetheless, society dictates performance or even acting at certain points, in order to be polite. Take our standard greeting, "How are you?" The cultural norm is to answer, "Good," or "Fine," regardless of feeling. Just last week, I carelessly asked my grandfather this question, when I knew he was not fine because my grandmother was in the hospital. Rather than saying, "Awful, and thanks for reminding me," he mumbled a socially acceptable, performance-based answer that camouflaged his thoughts, despite the fact that he cares little for social graces. These little concessions are necessary for society to function.

For members of the clergy and their families, this pressure to meet social expectation is amplified: The pastor has to preach, the wife to mingle with the flock, and the children to impersonate cherubim. However, the lives of pastors who have affairs seem to regularly show the same pattern; they get so lost in performing that they stop being and eventually just start to act. Sins take root in their lives, but because they are absorbed in acting like a Christian rather than being Christ-like, they fail to address issues of the heart. Thus, their struggles spiral out of control. This is likely why James admonished believers to "confess your sins to each other and pray for each other so that you may be healed."[7] Nothing kills sin like confession, but there is no confession without transparency.

For the children of pastors or missionaries, this quandary is more complicated. A PK or an MK is expected to act like a Christian in the midst of establishing his own faith which means performing or acting precede being out of necessity. However, just trying to grasp faith as a child is difficult enough; children often misconstrue what they hear. I remember once hearing the story of Moses and the Israelites crossing the Red Sea. When it came time to color a picture depicting the scene, I colored the water red. Why wouldn't I? They said it was the Red Sea.

A missionary or pastor's kid has to figure out how to be a follower of Christ internally when those changes may be imperceptible to those who aren't paying close attention or can't see through the lenses of performing and acting. Because he's expected to behave a certain way, it's difficult for the child to seek help in regards to his interior. Many children of the clergy, myself included, grow up as whitewashed tombs—clean on the outside but full of dead men's bones on the inside.

In the midst of all this, there were some people who saw beyond the performance and the acting in my life. There was one mission's pastor, by the name of Dr. Dairel O'Bar, who on at least one occasion perceived that I was disgruntled, struggling with my own Christian journey. He took me to breakfast, where we talked honestly about my life. Unfortunately, our interactions were not extensive as I now wish they had been.

Likewise, there was a widow in the church, Doris Howard, who saw me as an individual as well as a part of a missionary family. When she'd ask about how things were, she would listen

---

[7] James 5:16

for an answer and not be offended if the picture I painted wasn't pristine. Doris would say about me, "Whenever I ask Luke how things are going, he tells the truth."

If there was a perfect time for me to abandon all semblances of faith, it would have been college. After two years of junior college, I transferred to the University of Kansas, where I had one, or maybe two, Christian professors throughout my upperclassman education. Yet even as I took classes where I listened to instructors challenge Christianity, conviction sank in deep. As I sat in Women's History, read Nietzsche, or listened to faculty ridicule the idea of a creator, I was reminded of the words of the psalmist:

> Where can I go from your Spirit?
> Where can I flee from your presence?
> If I go to the heavens, you are there;
> if I make my bed in the depths, you are there.
> If I rise on the wings of the dawn,
> if I settle on the far side of the sea
> even there your hand will guide me,
> your right hand will hold me fast.
> If I say, "surely darkness will hide me
> and the light become night around me,"
> even the darkness will not be dark to you;
> the night will shine like the day
> for darkness is as light to you.[8]

It didn't take long for me to recognize what I'd already experienced throughout my life: God was real. Despite the professors and classmates who objected to and sometimes berated my beliefs, doubt was never able to displace God. It was as if a

[8] Psalm 139:7-12

person had come to me and insisted that my sister, Anna, was not real. My entire life I have known her; she's practically been a parent to me. Of course, Anna is a woman, so I can't claim to fully understand her or all her past actions. However, I can give account after account of our experiences, testify to her tastes and desires, and describe how she has influenced the lives of others. It's the same with God.

I still struggled with my faith, finding my desire to do right paired with sin at work in me. I fought with guilt and fear and loneliness, even divine silence, sometimes for months on end. Over time a new realization began to form; I told myself years before that I would obey God, whatever He asked, inanely claiming that I lived my life surrendered to Christ, and that I would follow whatever command I was given. It was a lie. I was withholding portions of my life from His control. For instance, until my senior year of college, I never trusted God enough to take a Sabbath; I never had the faith that He could provide in six days what I thought I needed a full seven days to accomplish.

In the midst of all the performing and acting while growing up, it was difficult for me to understand that the Christian life is a process of growth in which we are loved by God as we grow, just as a father and mother love their imperfect children throughout their maturation. Parents don't start loving their kids once they become adults; they love them at all stages of development. Based on my experience in the church, I thought I could only be loved based on my virtue. As a result, I wrestled with the idea that God could love me in the midst of my sinful behavior.

That's the beauty of the gospel, though; the Bible is full of imperfect people, people God loved in the midst of their imperfection. Certainly, He cared about them too much to allow them to wallow in destructive behavior, but His concern preceded any transformation. This is one of the major areas where

Christianity breaks with other religions; they are based around us fixing ourselves so we can approach God. Christianity, however, is about being reconciled to God and having a relationship with Him as He fixes us. As Paul wrote in Philippines 1:6, "He who began a good work in you will carry it on to completion until the day of Christ Jesus."

In the midst of life, I'm not perfect. I'm still prone to viewing my value as tied to my utility. Even as an adult, I live at times with a dogged sense of guilt, a feeling that I don't measure up, that I'm not doing enough for God, and that I'm not worthy of love. But God is teaching me differently. Now I don't hide myself; I'm real with the joy and pain which is how it should be. As I once heard it put, "If Christians are transparent, people will be less impressed with Christians and more impressed with God."

Grace

I know a family that went overseas in order to do mission work whose experience was disastrous. The couple's relationship was plagued by problems: verbal abuse, manipulation, depression, emotional unfaithfulness. Their funding was never adequate. The wife did not want to live abroad in the first place, but her husband didn't listen. They went abroad without the backing of a mission agency, and might not have been accepted by one had they applied.

Their family struggles were accentuated by issues like culture shock. After many years, they returned to America where their challenges continued. Alcoholism and an attempted suicide compounded the existing struggles before a divorce ended the marriage. In the years that followed, most of the children married only to fail in their respective relationships; one son and his children were abandoned by his wife while another son divorced his wife and embraced a homosexual lifestyle. Several of the kids rejected faith in God entirely.

It's valid to question whether the problems that festered were part of prior wounds that existed long before the transition from the U.S. to the foreign mission field. It makes sense to wonder if this couple should have been leading any kind of ministry in the first place. After all, one of the earliest admonitions about church leadership is that elders and deacons must manage their homes in exemplary fashions. Still, the reality remains that mission work is dangerous, and no amount of caution and preparation can eliminate all the risks.

During my family's time in the Philippines, we dealt with diseases, fires, theft, stalkers, home invasion, typhoons, hepatitis, amoeba, juvenile rheumatoid arthritis, and had multiple family members hospitalized throughout our tenure as we faced the fear of diseases like rabies and dengue fever—to say nothing of minor concerns like broken bones, lacerations, dog bites, cobras, and pythons—all while we lived as an ethnic minority in a foreign culture with seventy different languages, a tumultuous government, and multiple terrorist organizations, in addition to corrupt cops and politicians, who often had to be bribed—excuse me, given a gift—simply so that they would follow the letter of the law, and an army that was more concerned with siesta time than justice. As a college classmate once told me, I grew up in a James Bond movie.

Additionally, the life of a missionary is not just filled with physical threats; it's filled with spiritual dangers as well. The Bible describes an invisible world existing along with ours that is in the midst of an eternal conflict where the angels of God battle the forces of Satan. From Genesis, the tone of the fight has been set: the offspring of the woman would crush the serpent's head, and the serpent would strike His heel. The outcome has never been in doubt, but wounds are guaranteed. It is no wonder that even the apostle Paul admitted despairing of life at points in his missionary journeys.

My family's time in the Philippines or back in the United States on furloughs wasn't all beaches and exotic food, and some trials lasted for months, injuring the spirits of those involved. There were moments when evil probed deep into my own life or the lives of my family members, causing destruction and wounds that have taken years to mend. Even after healing, the scars remain. Some of the stories are simply too personal to share, but I don't hesitate to acknowledge that such realities exist.

In some ways, my family's attitude in the Philippines mimicked that of Shadrach, Meshach, and Abednego when they stood before the king of Babylon, faced with the decision to worship the golden image or be thrown into the furnace. They responded, "If we are thrown into the blazing furnace, the God we serve is able to save us from it, and he will rescue us from your hand, O king. But even if he does not, we want you to know, O king, that we will not serve your gods or worship the image of gold you have set up."[9] My family's time abroad was not without flames that licked against the walls of our home, and there was an understanding that we live, and sometimes die, by the grace of God.

Over the years, I've reflected on how even death—an earthly, human death—is a matter of divine grace: death is a gift. The picture in Genesis is simple enough; God told Adam that he could eat any fruit in the Garden of Eden except for the fruit from the tree of the knowledge of good and evil, saying, "For when you eat from it you will surely die."[10] We know that the death God spoke of could not have solely been physical human death because Adam did not immediately die after eating the forbidden fruit; instead he lived on for hundreds of years. There was an immediate spiritual death, though, as Adam immediately started fearing the presence of God; the relationship between God and man was sundered.

In this state of broken fellowship, speaking within the Trinity, God said, "The man has now become like one of us, knowing good and evil. He must not be allowed to reach out his hand and take also from the tree of life and eat, and life forever."[11] If

---

[9] Daniel 3:17-18

[10] Genesis 2:17

[11] Genesis 3:22

man had been allowed to live infinitely, without physical death, reconciliation with God in its entirety would never have been possible. Certainly because of Jesus' death as payment for our sin, full reconciliation is possible by grace through faith, yet the full reunion lies not on this earth but in the next. Without death, humans would be trapped in lives filled with pain and suffering for eternity. But because of the grace of physical human death, those trials are limited to a season.

While we were in the Philippines, my family saw grace in less dramatic ways as well. When Mom was pregnant with me, she went into labor six weeks early. She was checked into the hospital where the doctors gave her an intravenous medication that suppressed the contractions. Eventually they tried to switch my mother from the intravenous drug to an oral drug, but every time they did, Mom went back into full-scale labor. After days filled with unsuccessful attempts to stop the labor, my father called our primary supporting church and asked them to pray. It just so happened that his call came during one of the church services, so during the service the pastor shared our need with the congregation and led them in prayer. The next time the physicians tried to switch my mother's medication, they succeeded, and she was able to go to our mission home.

There were also the moments that my parents knew nothing about. In our first several years in the Philippines, my family lived in Naga City, as did another missionary family, the Zulls, who had four children stair-stepped in age with my older siblings and me. The kids all enjoyed having peers of their own age and nationality—I probably enjoyed this relationship less than some of my siblings as the Zull girl who was around my age was bigger than me and used to pull out my hair; I blame my high forehead on her.

For whatever reason, the parents decided that their kids should only play together a couple of times a week, though the eldest kids felt this rule was ridiculous. Anna and Caleb took to getting out of bed at four in the morning, sneaking out of the house, and riding their bikes to meet the eldest Zull kids who had likewise slipped out. They would play together for an hour and then return home before the parents awoke. This became a daily occurrence in a country and city where there were regular kidnappings, thefts, and assaults. Anna and Caleb were stealthy enough about the operation that my parents never caught on, only finding out when Anna told them a few years ago.

Even beyond simply surviving, and ideally thriving, while living in the Philippines, our family had to trust that somehow God would use us to reach the Filipino population with the gospel, often despite our own ineptitude. Even the best intentions could lead to horrible, sometimes comic, failure. During our time in the Philippines, one of our katulongs, Larry, grew sick of the constant trouble she had with her teeth; eventually she had them all removed and switched to dentures. One day Hosanna stole Larry's teeth, promising to hold them hostage until our beloved katulong converted to Christianity. Thankfully, Larry was gracious enough to overlook the incident. I can only imagine how many other similar stories exist when my family trespassed in our zeal.

As long as I can remember, Dad has quoted the first couple verses of Psalm 127:

> Unless the LORD builds the house
>   the builders labor in vain.
> Unless the Lord watches over the city,
>   the guards stand watch in vain.
> In vain you rise early
>   and stay up late,
> toiling for food to eat—
>   for he grants sleep to those he loves.

These words were repeated with the intent of reminding my family that no amount of human effort can ensure success, whether in evangelism, or support development, or raising a family. There is no benefit to diligently building sandcastles when the tide is encroaching. At the same time, working in sync with a cosmic force can turn a word into an avalanche. With God, sometimes knowing how to drive a tent peg or use a slingshot or sing is more effective than leading an army; victory often comes through the mundane.

For the longest time, Dad would stop after quoting verses one and two, and he wrestled with understanding how the last four verses of Psalm 127 related to the previous two because there is such a sudden switch in topic:

> Children are a heritage from the LORD,
>   offspring a reward from him.
> Like arrows in the hands of a warrior
>   are children born in one's youth.
> Blessed is the man
>   whose quiver is full of them.
> They will not be put to shame
>   when they contend with their opponents in court.

Over the years, my father has started quoting these last verses because they speak to his awakening value for large families. Family is an extremely ordinary aspect of life. Children aren't flashy; they're noisy and expensive and messy. They're easy to underestimate and undervalue. Yet the potential for children to shape the world is enormous; like rain drips falling into a pool, they alter the face of the water.

There are moments when I have the arrogance to attribute the success of my family to us. In reality, the comparative triumphs of my family aren't due to the things we did—the discipline, the sacrifice, the love—though those things helped. What made the difference was grace, unmerited favor. There's now an awareness in my family that our actions ultimately do not control our lives; there's a bigger force at work who makes His plans and determines ours, often regardless of human intentions.

Though I don't pretend to have a perfect understanding of the paradoxical relationship between God's sovereignty and man's responsibility, I can say one thing with certainty: It's by the grace of God that my family turned out the way we did and that we were protected as much as we were. Despite fires and hurricanes and trials, I am grateful.

Something New

There's a basic reality about arrows: they don't stay put. They are made to travel far distances, sometimes with drastic impacts; they may return to the quiver for a time, but they don't stay in place for long. If my siblings are, as my parents often quote, "arrows in the hands of a warrior," it's fitting that my family is dispersing. Children don't stay children forever.

By the time my family returned from the Philippines, Anna was already married and living with her husband in Wichita. He was also a missionary kid and works in aeronautics, having fallen in love with flying at a young age. They're currently expecting their sixth child and continue to consider foreign work opportunities with David's company.

Likewise Caleb had finished his degree in electrical engineering at the University of Kansas and took a job in Kansas City. In time he met his wife, Whitney. As an only child, she found integrating into our large family a bit of a shock but a welcome change. They've been married for nearly three years now.

Shortly after my family returned stateside, Enoch left to attend Prairie Bible Institute in Canada. My parents observed that if he went to school in Canada, he might meet a Canadian girl. Sure enough, Enoch soon met his Canadian wife, Andrea. Six years after their marriage, they are expecting their third child and are returning to the Philippines to be dorm parents at Faith Academy, a school for missionary kids.

The rest of the currently-unmarried siblings—though that number is once again threatened—all still live in Wichita for the time being. Esther is through college and engaged. Nathan is a medic with the Army Reserves and did a tour in the Greater Middle East. Josiah, after a couple mission trips to the Philippines and Mozambique, is leaving for school in the United Kingdom. Meanwhile, Abigail is starting junior college, and Hosanna is finishing high school.

For my part, after graduating with my degree in English with an emphasis in Creative Writing, I interned with Campus Crusade for Christ for a year, including a summer project in Juneau, Alaska. I worked a temporary job as the interim manager for a mini storage business in Chanute for a while. Afterwards, I spent a month with my family in Wichita before traveling to Asheville, North Carolina where there's a young church I'm interested in—I confess this move also put me in closer proximity to my fiancée who is finishing her Master's degree in Literature at Liberty University. I've lived in five cities over the last two years. Working lets me write, and perhaps someday writing will be my work.

As for my parents, they're still missionaries with International Student's Incorporated in Wichita. Their work with foreign students is the most vibrant ministry I've seen them in. When they first began working with ISI, they started praying that every week someone in their ministry would accept Jesus. The rest of their team thought that prayer was overly ambitious, but my parents kept praying. Then almost two years ago, more people accepted Christ than there were weeks in the school year, and this rate has continued. Not long ago, one of their friends said, "Well, it's time to start praying for two students a week now."

As far as kids go though, the nest is emptying. It won't be long now before all of us children will be adults starting families of our own. Each year, the size of our family grows, and just fitting into one location is increasingly tricky. When my parents bought a house again, they expanded the dining room out an additional eight feet to hold their expanding family; five years later, we've already outgrown the expansion. In a few more years, we'll almost need a hotel for family gatherings; in a decade, there may not be any other option.

At present, my family, including spouses, grandchildren, and my fiancée, totals twenty-five people. The number is growing all the time, and sometimes it's a little difficult to keep abreast of the numbers. A few weeks ago, I was sitting in my parents' kitchen with Abigail—my fiancée Abigail, not my sister Abigail (big families get confusing, I know). Mom and Enoch were chatting nearby when Mom mentioned Enoch's two kids. Then she stopped and corrected herself: three kids, not two kids. Abigail and I looked at each other questioningly before asking, "Wait. Hold on a second. Three kids? Did we miss something?"

"Oh, yeah," Enoch said, "Didn't anyone tell you? Andrea's pregnant with number three."

Everything is an adventure when you're a child, but as kids grow up, Neverland, that childhood dreamland, fades into the distance. Still, children aren't the only ones who have adventures. After growing up in the Philippines and returning home, it'd be easy to assume that life would sink back into the ordinary and mundane, that nothing about the everyday could be as exciting or dramatic or entertaining. However, that simply isn't true. The adventure continues, and even the mundane can amuse and instruct if viewed correctly.

Adulthood is bittersweet. Watching my siblings and I fly further apart is a somber occurrence, but there are new joys as well. There's the imminent approach of marriage and parenthood. I've been reminded of most of the new experiences awaiting me while observing Anna, Caleb, and Enoch as they've ventured into the realms of marriage and parenthood. There are more than a few tales there to be told, more than I can recall or pass on, though I will share some, knowing that in time I too will have stories to add.

David recounts one early morning when he and Anna were awakened not by noise, but by quiet. Silence can be a terrifying thing when you have children waking early in the morning because, if you can hear the noise, you can monitor their activities and assess the casualties from afar. Quiet is a portent of doom. On this particular morning, awakened by the calm, they ventured out of their room and discovered the bathroom door open and their boys, Jonathan and Marcus—three and two years old respectively—standing beside the toilet with the lid open. The porcelain throne was filled with urine and feces and toilet paper. Apparently, the boys had realized that they added too much paper, so they were scooping contents from the bowl. The fetid amalgamation was everywhere, the boys' clothes were covered, and the floor was a swamp.

David turned to Anna quickly and said, "I'll clean it up."

He picked Jonathan and Marcus up one at a time and placed them in the bathtub. They could see his consternation; the room was somber.

Then Jonathan spoke hopefully, "Daddy, Jesus died to take our punishment, right?"

David looked at the two of them quietly and finally said, "Yes, Jonathan, that's correct." Then he cleaned them up and sent them on without punishment, knowing that sometimes teaching truth is more important than teaching responsibility.

With each additional child, Anna and David have had more trials and more laughter. Each kid is a bundle of personality:

Jonathan the stubborn older brother, Marcus the mold breaker with a knack for saying inappropriate things—he takes after me—Esther Brianna the only girl, Elijah the surprisingly eloquent two year old, and baby Peter.

As the only girl, Bria persists in asking for sisters and was recently heard praying, "God, put babies in there (Anna's tummy)." Later she added, "Come out now?" and "It's taking a long time." On another occasion, I heard her pray for sisters with the concession that, "Another brother would be alright too."

Not long ago, the children caught a case of stomach flu and passed it from one to the other and back and forth with the kind of openhandedness that parents usually encourage amongst their children. For weeks, Anna and David were up every night with one child or more who had awakened with an upset stomach and vomit everywhere. Unlike most stomach sickness, this particular strain was strangely paired with a strong appetite. Eventually, the doctor advised that the children be limited to a liquid diet and a few crackers. Though the older kids understood the restriction, Bria and Elijah did not.

Unhappy with her strict diet, Bria, who had received a Bible for Christmas, came to David with it and said, "You're not being kind. Read."

David pretended to read and quoted, "Children, obey your parents in the Lord for this is right."

Bria didn't like that, so she turned to a different spot and demanded, "Read."

David quoted, "Honor your father and mother, so that you may live long in the land I am giving you."

Bria didn't approve of that answer either, so she flipped to a different spot and repeated, "Read."

This time David finally read the verse before him. It was about a young man who didn't obey, so God put him to death.

At that, Bria slammed her Bible shut and stomped off.

As I look to the future, in the midst of all the responsibilities of the family that I see coming, there are the questions. There's the matter of family size, the issues about how to educate, and the complications of teaching children about sex in a world with such different ideals. In the midst of it all, parenting is as amateur a sport as ever. Yet, I see on the horizon how consistently blessings and challenges are intertwined, one allowing for or magnifying the other. There's an almost illogical relationship between joy and stress while raising a family. But in the midst of it all, there's growth.

Bibliography

Pride, Mary. *The Way Home: Beyond Feminism and Back to Reality.* Westchester, Illinois: Crossway Books, a division of Good News Publishers, 1985.

CPSIA information can be obtained at www.ICGtesting.com
Printed in the USA
BVOW07s0612220115

384376BV00001B/2/P

9 781490 858753